SCOTLAND'S WEATHER

An anthology

D1003286

SCOTLAND'S
WEATHER
An anthology

Compiled by Andrew Martin

NATIONAL MUSEUMS OF SCOTLAND

Published by the National Museums of Scotland,
Chambers Street, Edinburgh EH1 1JF
© Trustees of the National Museums of Scotland 1995
Introduction © Anita McConnell 1995

All rights reserved. Except as permitted under current legis-
lation no part of this publication may be reproduced, stored
in a retrieval system or transmitted, in any form or by any
means, electronic, mechanical, photocopying, recording or
otherwise, without the prior permission of the publisher.

British Library Cataloguing in Publication Data
A catalogue record of this book is available from the British
Library

ISBN 0 948636 71 8

Designed by the Publications Office, National Museums of
Scotland
Printed in Great Britain by Clifford Press Ltd, Coventry

Acknowledgements

The Publisher and Editor wish to thank the following for permission to reprint copyright material in this
anthology:

Carcanet Press Ltd for Hugh MacDiarmid *To Circumjack Cencrastus* from Complete Poems; Chapman and Joan Lennon for
Words for Snow; Chapman and Donald C Farquhar for *Sheddaes*; Chatto & Windus for Jessie Kesson *Where the Apple Ripens* and
George Mackay Brown *Greenvoe*; George Anderson Clarke *Deskford Parish*; Colonel John Clavering for Molly Clavering *From the
Border Hills*; Curtis Brown for Ronald Frame *Paris* from *Watching Mrs Gordon and other stories*, copyright © Ronald Frame 1987;
Andre Deutsch Ltd for Denis Forman *Son of Adam* 1990; Duckworth for R B Cunninghame Graham A *Hatchment*; Faber and
Faber Ltd for Edwin Muir *Scotland's Winter* from *Collected Poems*; Buff Hardie *Scottish Weather*; Nick Hern Books for Tony Roper
The Steamie; Robin Jenkins *The Cone Gatherers*; R L C Lorimer and the Trustees of the W L Lorimer Memorial Trust Fund for *The
New Testament in Scots* tr W L Lorimer © R L C Lorimer 1983; Gavin Maxwell Enterprises Ltd for Gavin Maxwell *The House of
Elrig* © Gavin Maxwell Enterprises 1965; Methuen for H V Morton *In Search of Scotland* © Reed Consumer Books Ltd; Dr
Elizabeth Michie for Nancy Brysson Morrison *The Gowk Storm*; John Murray (Publishers) Ltd for Jane and Mary Findlater
Crossriggs; Oxford University Press for Otta Swire *Skye: the Island and its Legends* 1952; Polygon for Maud Sulter *No Oxbridge Spires*,
A L Kennedy *Tea and Biscuits* from *Night Geometry and the Garscadden Trains*, Lewis Grassic Gibbon *The Speak o' the Mearns*,
Elizabeth Burns *Valda's Poem / Sleevenotes* from *Ophelia and Other Poems*; Random House UK Limited for Norman MacCaig *Small
Rain* and *Cold Wind in May*;

and the following for assistance in tracing material:

Aberdeen & North East Scotland Family History Society; Elizabeth Burns; Canongate Publishing Ltd; Ewart Library,
Dumfries; Highland Region Libraries, Inverness and Portree; Lang Syne Publishers; Graham C Hunter, Ledingham Chalmers;
Longman Group; Tom Martin; Penguin Books; Polygon; Ramsay Head Press; Dr Bo Schoene; The Scotsman; Society of
Antiquaries of Scotland; Jane Swire; Tarossay Castle; Virago; Dr Christopher Whyte;

and especially our colleagues in the National Museums of Scotland who provided so many ideas and suggestions,
and the NMS Photographic Service.

Every effort has been made to trace the copyright owners of the works included in this anthology. If any error
or oversight has occurred the Publisher would be grateful for information, and will correct any such errors at
the earliest opportunity.

Illustration acknowledgements for pages:
75, 91, 99: City of Edinburgh Art Centre. 78: © HIE. 86, Scottish Highland Photo Library. Otherwise all illustrations are the
copyright of the photographer or artist specified, or the NMS.

Front cover: *Suilvan, Wester Ross.* Douglas Corrance
Inside covers: *Raindrops in a birch tree.* Laurie Campbell
Frontispiece: *Rainbow over Loch Ness.* Douglas Corrance

Bi gu subhach, geamnaidh,
Moch-tràthach a's t-Samhradh;
Bi gu curraiceach, brògach,
Brochanachc's a' Gheamhradh.

In summer time be cheerful, chaste,
And early out of bed;
In Winter be well-capped, well-shod,
And well on porridge fed.

Gaelic proverb

Introduction

Seen from space, ours is a blue planet, wreathed in clouds which move across its disc, continuously forming and dissolving. North and south of the Equator are zones of travelling eddies or spirals, which are formed when warm tropical air meets cold air from the polar regions. Scotland lies under the zone of eddies in the northern hemisphere, and the variability of Scotland's weather owes much to their passage over the region.

Whilst we cannot see the wind, its course is marked by the clouds it bears along. The eddies that sweep over Scottish skies bring air from all quarters in turn. A glance at the atlas shows that air from the west or southwest has passed over the vast Atlantic Ocean which reaches Scotland's west coast. Air from the north will have traversed the Arctic Ocean which washes the Shetlands, Orkneys and Scotland's northern coast. That from the east and south will have passed over continental Europe and perhaps crossed the North Sea before reaching Scotland's east coast.

Each wind brings its own characteristic weather, according to the season. The Atlantic Ocean is always relatively warm, so moist westerly winds bring most of Scotland's rain, which falls principally on the western margins of the country. The north winds of summer cross a chilly Arctic Ocean and bring noticeably colder weather, often with light rain or showers. In winter, when parts of the northern seas are frozen, the air can be extremely cold and dry, giving remarkable visibility. Winds from the east and south, having travelled over land, can be warm and dry in summer, cold and dry in winter, although winds passing over the North Sea can pick up enough moisture to drop considerable amounts of rain or snow on Scotland's eastern counties.

The amount of moisture which air can absorb as it crossed open water increases with its temperature. The western winds are the warmest and the most moisture-laden. As these winds reach the coast, the air must rise to cross the mountains. As air rises, it cools, the moisture condenses, clouds form, bringing heavy rain along the coast with snow at higher levels. The western part of

Looking towards Rhum.

Scotland receives around three times more precipitation than the eastern part where the air is generally drier.

The famous Scottish mist consists of cloud at ground level, formed of drops of moisture so small that they hang in the air and cling to any vegetation as individual droplets. On days when rain showers alternate with sunny periods, rainbows are a common sight.

Scotland lies between latitudes of 55° and 61° North, and while the summer days are long, the sun is never high in the sky. In winter the sun rises only a little way above the horizon and sinks again within a few hours. This low sun angle, which causes the rays of light to pass through a considerable thickness of the atmosphere, is responsible for many of the optical effects and colours of the sky and clouds which artists and visitors find so attractive.

Some passages in this anthology describe weather more extreme than we are now accustomed to. In historical times written records supplement archaeological evidence of warmth increasing from around 800 to 1300AD, when the treeline and the limits of cultivation stood higher than they do now. Towards the end of this period, however, there are records of severe storms, flooding along low coasts and notable droughts, and a period of gradual cooling set in. These events were naturally reflected in the lives of the people, and also on the plants and animals of the region. A dreadful run of wet summers between 1313 and 1320 resulted in crop failure, with people and animals ravaged by starvation and disease.

In the 1430s came a series of extremely severe winters. The long history of clan raids and cattle stealing from the lowlands must owe something to the stress of a deteriorating climate after the golden age of maximum settlement and cultivation enjoyed during the twelfth and thirteenth centuries. On various occasions between 1200 and 1800 southerly gales struck the east coast during low tide, sweeping vast quantities of sand inland, and in several cases fertile fields or settlements were entirely buried. A notable example is the medieval town of Forvie, on the east coast of Aberdeenshire, overwhelmed in August 1413.

During the 'Little Ice Age' of the sixteenth to eighteenth centuries the ocean surface northeast of Scotland was some 5°C cooler than now and the weather coming from that direction was markedly colder. Travellers reported permanent snow on the Cairngorms. Cold winters may be tolerable providing food supplies hold out, but late frosts which damage crops in the growing season, and low summer temperatures which prevent ripening inevitably bring famine and loss of livestock in their wake. Such disasters struck with increasing frequency and severity up to 1700.

Since then there has been a slow improvement, albeit with occasional regressions. In recent centuries people began to take advantage of winter's ice and snow. The sports of skating and curling became popular whenever the weather allowed, followed more recently by ski resorts opening in parts of the Highlands which could anticipate a reasonable snow cover.

These climatic changes account for some of the apparent anomalies in popular weather lore. In fact, these sayings fall into two groups: those which forecast weather, and those which forecast climate. Climatic forecasts, those sayings which predict summer rainfall from observing when species of tree come into leaf, or severity of the coming winter from the time of migration of certain birds, have little validity. But familiarity with the local topography can enable a reasonable forecast of weather within the next few hours to be made, if the wind direction, temperature and humidity are known. The observer without instruments takes information from the form and height of the clouds, and the visibility and colour of the sky. Over hundreds, or thousands, of years, people have recorded these weather signs in the form of proverbs, such as the familiar 'red sky at night...'

This anthology reflects the amazing variety of Scotland's weather, moving from ice and snow through rain, storm and mist to burning days with brilliant sunshine. The reality can be a long way from Buff Hardie's description of the seasons in the first piece, Scottish Weather!

Anita McConnell

Rughadh shuas an ám laidhe,
Dh' éireadh Fionn moch's a' mhaduinn;
Rughadh shuas's a'mhoch mhaduinn,
Dheanadh Fionn an ath-chadal.

With a rosy sky at bed-time,
Fingal would rise early,
With a rosy sky at dawn
He would take another sleep.

Gaelic proverb

Valentine's   *Donal (to English tourist): "I doot we're goin to hae a shoo'r."*   Series 158

Scottish Weather
(Efter Michael Flanders)

January without fail
Brings tae Scotland sleet and hail;
February's bad an' a' –
Sauchiehall Street deep in sna'.

March's gales mak a'body chilled;
The wind gings whistlin' up yer kilt.
April showers? No, much worse, oh!
Poorin' rain fae Troon tae Thurso.

May brings frost; it mak's ye greet –
Kills the floo'rs in Princes Street.
June's that bleak yer face is blue;
Half o' Falkirk's doon wi' flu.

July is weet for the Glesca Fair –
Deep depression everywhere:
Sodden picnics, trippers sad;
When August comes it's twice as bad.

In September fog and mist
Mak' ye feel like gettin' drunk.
October ice; yer car, by God,
Gings skitin' aff the Rhynie road.

November brings a change, that's richt –
Rain a' day an' sna a' nicht.
December's ten times worse, and then
January's back again.

Buff Hardie (Scotland the What), b1931

Scotland's Winter

Now the ice lays its smooth claws on the sill,
The sun looks from the hill
Helmed in his winter casket,
And sweeps his arctic sword across the sky.
The water at the mill
Sounds more hoarse and dull.
The miller's daughter walking by
With frozen fingers soldered to her basket
Seems to be knocking
Upon a hundred leagues of floor
With her light heels, and mocking
Percy and Douglas dead,
And Bruce on his burial bed,
Where he lies white as may
With wars and leprosy,
And all the kings before
This land was kingless,
And all the singers before
This land was songless,
This land that with its dead and living waits the Judgement Day.
But they, the powerless dead,
Listening can hear no more
Than a hard tapping on the floor
A little overhead
Of common heels that do not know
Whence they come or where they go
And are content
With their poor frozen life and shallow banishment.

Edwin Muir, 1887-1959

If Candlemas Day be fair and clear
The half o' winter's to gang an' mair.
If Candlemas Day be dark and foul
The half o' winter's past at Yule.

Traditional

from The Testament of Cresseid

Ane doolie sessoun to ane cairfull dyte
Suld correspond, and be equivalent.
Richt sa it wes quhen I began to wryte
This tragedie, the wedder richt fervent
Quhen Aries in middis of the Lent;
Schouris of haill can fra the north discend,
That scantlie fra the cauld I micht defend.

* * *

The northin wind had purifyit the air,
And shed the misty cloudis fra the sky;
The frost freisit, the blastis bitterly
Fra Pole Artick come quhisling loud and schill,
And causit me remufe aganis my will.

* * *

I mend the fyre and beikit me about,
Then tuik ane drink my spreitis to comfort,
And armit me weill fra the cauld thairout;
To cut the winter nicht and mak it schort,
I tuik ane quair, and left all uther sport,
Writtin be worthy Chaucer glorious,
Of fair Cresseid, and worthie Troylus.

Robert Henryson, 1420-1490

Black sun of winter. *Slate mosaic on panel, inspired by the Orkney landscape.* George Garson 1980

Snow on whisky casks, Speyside. Dave Reed

from An Itinerary Containing his Ten Yeeres' Travell

Scotland reaching so farre into the North, must needs be subject to excessive cold, yet the same is in some sort mitigated by the thicknesse of the cloudy aire and sea vapours. And as in the Northerne parts of England, they have small plessantnes, goodnesse or abundance of Fruites and Flowers, so in Scotland they have much lesse, or none at all. And I remember, that coming to Barwick in the moneth of May, wee had great stormes, and felt great cold, when for two moneths before, the pleasant Spring had smiled on us at London.

Fynes Moryson, 1566-1617

On a Heavy Fall of Snow

The men o' the east
Are pykin their geese,
And sendin' their feathers here away, here away.

Traditional

47 Words for Snow

The Inuit, or so I've heard,
have more than 47 words
for snow.
A furry gauntlet has been flung,
a challenge I accept.
There is, to start,
wind-wailing snow, and silent in the night,
the fat-and-lazy kind, and hiding under shrubs
There's almost-rain,
ice-muffler, and old ladies' fright
There's seldom by the sea snow
and cats won't pee in it,
white in the light, indigo in the shadows,
and sudden squall blots out Dundee
There's birdculling snow, branch-snapper,
quiet coat, and buryer of bulbs
There's grey over water
snow that can barely etch the grass,
slate-sliding, sledge-happy snow
kamakazi at the windscreen,
lighting up the night,
the strange, seductive, wet-nosed kisses kind
There's snow waiting, weighty in the forest,
blown from the hillside,
gone by noon

The challenge stands and I succumb.
The Inuit have me outdone
by 21.

Joan Lennon, b1953

from A Modern Account of Scotland
by an English Gentleman

The judgement of hail and snow is natural-
ized and made free denison here, and continues with them from the sun's first ingress
into Aries, till he has passed the 30th degree
of Aquary.

    The vallies for the most part are cov-
ered with beer or bigg, and the hills with
snow; and as in the northern countries the
bears and foxes change their coats into the
livery of the soyl; so there the moor fowl
(called termagants) turn white, to sute the
sample, though the inhabitants still stand to
their Ægyptian hue.

               Thomas Kirke, 1650-1706

Ptarmigan in the snow. Laurie Campbell

*Sledging in the lunch hour at Dalwhinnie School,
Inverness-shire, December 1935.* Keystone, SEA

from The Brave Days

It's a sheer illusion, I suppose, But I can never get over the idea that winters up till 1895 were always frosty, with lochs and ponds everywhere bearing, and that skating up till then was a national pastime every child had indulged in as naturally as in bools and peever, fishing for baggy-minnows, trundling a hoop, shinty, or hide-and-seek.

There really must have been ample opportunities for skating in old-time Scotland, for in the eighteenth century the best skaters in Europe were to be found in Edinburgh, and the oldest skating club in existence was founded there in 1778. The British Encyclopedia a hundred years ago said; 'The metropolis of Scotland has produced more instances of elegant skaters than perhaps any other country whatsoever.'

Not till February, 1895, however, did I recover the first fine careless rapture of that marvellous winter on Loch Fyne, when even the stags went skating. February had opened with filled dykes of snow, followed by an ardent frost that settled down to make a banner year of it in the grand old style. In less than a week the domestic water-taps of Glasgow were frozen solid, and householders had to get their supplies from street wells hastily extemporized by tapping the mains. There was great distress among the poor in the city: for their relief the Lord Provost raised a fund of £8000 in ten days.

It was, undoubtedly, the coldest weather experienced in Scotland for thirty-five years, and Loch Lomond was frozen over and bearing by February 16. On that day I skated between Balloch and Inchmurrin. Special trains were run from Queen Street to Balloch, and 30,000 people were on the ice.

Four days later David Hodge and I made for Balloch again, to find even greater numbers disporting themselves on ice which was now much safer. Booths, tents, and huxters' barrows lined the shore between the railway and Cameron House; a roaring business was being done in the hiring and fixing of skates and hot coffee, but there was not a single cigarette to be got for love or money.

That frost lasted for more than a month; it was only on March 8 that gravitation water was restored to Glasgow houses. After four weeks of continuous ice the skating spirit was revived in Scotland, but not for long. It cannot be sustained at its best on artificial ice rinks or unresilient tarmac ponds.

Neil Munro, 1864-1930

Necropolis, Glasgow.

from In Search of Scotland

Suddenly the sunlight dies. I enter a mist: a thin, clinging mist, a cold foggy mist. I am warm with my climb. I do not notice how cold it is. Out of it emerge two shapes. Two men come towards me muffled to the eyes. They wear gloves and their teeth are chattering, their noses are red, their ears stand out like slices of raw beef. They try to smile but the smile freezes on their iced cheeks:

'Another half mile!' they say to me. 'Is it still fine down below?'

'Yes, brilliant sun!'

They swing their arms like cabmen on a frosty morning, and, taking off their gloves, blow into their cold fingers.

'Don't lean on the wooden platform over the ravine. It's not safe! Good-bye!'

And they depart, fading in the mist. As I go on the mist thickens. There are irregular patches of snow two or three inches deep. I have come into the depth of

Ben Nevis.

winter. An icy wind
howls round me, whip-
ping the chill mist into my face. All the
heat of my climb is taken out of me. I
stoop in the wind and take out a coat from
my knapsack and cover myself; but I am now so cold that I
cannot feel my ears; and my eyes ache.

The mist turns to sleet, and the sleet to soft, whirling snow
that dances giddily round me on every side. The path becomes level. Through the
snow I see the ruin of a stone house. I go in for shelter. It is a horrible ruin, like a
shipwreck. It looks as if all the fiends of the air have torn it stone from stone. I
hear the most horrible sound on earth – the sough of wind coming up over the

*Observatory station on
the summit of Ben Nevis.*

crest of Ben Nevis. It is not loud. I have to listen for it, and having heard it I go on listening with chilled blood: it is a dreadful sound; an evil, damnable sound. I am drawn towards it through the snow. I come to the jagged edge of the mountain. The snow is whirled up over the edge of it. It is as if the snow were rising and not falling; and all the time the wind comes moaning out of space over the edge of Ben Nevis.

The precipice is 1,500 feet deep. I take a stone and fling it. Seven sickening seconds and then, far off, an echo of the fall and another and another.

I stand chilled to the very marrow, watching the weird snowfall veer and shift in the wind, blowing aside to reveal dim, craggy shapes, rocks like spectres or crouching men or queer misshapen beasts. And the dreadful ghost of a wind moaning over the precipice with an evil invitation at the back of it, moaning up out of space, through distant spiky gullies where the sun is shining, moaning with a suggestion of inhuman mirth, causes me to face the ravine as if something might come out of it which would have to be fought.

I could stay there longer if the wind would not bite into my bones and numb my fingers. I go on out of the snow and into the sleet and the mist. And on my way down a great hole is suddenly blown in the cloud, and I see, it seems at my feet, an amazing, brilliant panorama of mountains with the sun on them, of blue lochs, a steamer no bigger than a fly moving up Loch Ness beneath the arch of a rainbow. Then the hole fills with mist and I go on for an hour, stumbling, scrambling until the mist frays and stops, and the sun shines...

All round me are the Highlands, magnificent among the clouds, the evening blueness spreading over them; peak calling to peak, the Atlantic like a thin streak of silver, the bare rock beneath my feet fading to brown bogland and heather.

H V Morton, 1892-1979

Meditatioun in Wyntir

In to thir dark and drublie dayis,
Quhone sabill all the hevin arrayis
With mystie vapouris, cluddis, and skyis
Nature all curage me denyis
Off sangis, ballattis, and of playis.

Quhone that the nycht dois lenthin houris,
With wind, with haill, and havy schouris,
My dule spreit dois lurk for schoir,
My hairt for languor dois forloir
For laik of symmer with his flouris.

I walk, I turne, sleip may I nocht,
I vexit am with havie thocht ;
This warld all ouir I cast about,
And ay the mair I am in dout,
The mair that I remeid have socht.

William Dunbar, c1456-1513

Glencoe. Douglas Corrance

[22]

These constitute the various aeras of the pastoral life. They are the red lines in the shepherd's manual – the remembrance of years and ages that are past – the tablets of memory by which the ages of his children the times of his ancestors and the rise and downfall of families are invariably ascertained. Even the progress of improvements in Scots farming can be traced traditionally from these, and the rent of a farm or estate given with precision, before and after such and such a storm, though the narrator be uncertain in what century the said notable storm happened. 'Mar's year' and 'that year the heelanders raide' are but secondary mementos to *the year Nine* and *the year Forty* – these stand in bloody capitals in the annals of the pastoral life as well as many more that shall hereafter be mentioned.

The most dismal of all those on record is *the Thirteen drifty days*. This extra-ordinary storm as near as I have been able to trace must have occurred in the year 1620. The traditionary stories and pictures of desolation that remain of it are the most dire imaginable and the mentioning of the thirteen drifty days to an old shepherd in a stormy winter night never fails to impress his mind with a sort of religious awe and often sets him on his knees before that Being who alone can avert such another calamity.

It is said that for thirteen days and nights the snow drift never once abated – the ground was covered with frozen snow when it commenced and during all that time the sheep never broke their fast. The cold was intense to a degree never before remembered and about the fifth and sixth days of the storm the young sheep began to fall into a sleepy and torpid state and all that were so affected in the evening died over night. The intensity of the frost wind often cut them off when in that state quite instantaneously. About the ninth and tenth days the shepherds began to build up huge semi-circular walls of their dead in order to afford some shelter for the remainder of the living but they availed but little for about the same time they were frequently seen tearing at one another's wool with their teeth.

When the storm abated, on the fourteenth day from its commencement, there was on many a high-lying farm not a living sheep to be seen. Large mishapen walls of dead, surrounding a small prostrate flock likewise all dead, and frozen stiff in their lairs, were all that remained to cheer the forlorn shepherd and his master and though on low-lying farms where the snow was not so hard before numbers of sheep weathered the storm yet their constitutions received such a shock that the greater part of them perished afterwards and the final consequence was that about nine tenths of all the sheep in the South of Scotland were destroyed.

In the extensive pastoral district of Eskdalemoor which maintains upwards of 20,000 sheep it is said none were left alive but forty young wedders on

Snowstorm in the Grampians.

one farm and five old ewes on another. The farm of Phaup remained without a stock and without a tenant for twenty years subsequent to the storm, at length one very honest and liberal minded man ventured to take a lease of it at the annual rent of *a grey coat and a pair of hose.*

James Hogg, 1770-1835

Aiteamh na gaoithe tuath, sneachd 'us reodhadh anns an uair.

After thaw with northern blast, snow and frost follow fast.

Gaelic proverb

Edinburgh in the snow.

from The Journal of Sir Walter Scott

31 January to 9 February 1831

Retain my purpose, however, and set out for Edinburgh alone – that is, no one but my servant. The snow became impassable, and in Edinburgh I remain immovably fixed for ten days – that is, till Wednesday – never once getting out of doors, save to dinner, when I went and returned in a sedan chair. I commenced my quarantine in Mackenzie's Hotel, where I was deadly cold, and it was tolerably noisy... The appearance of the streets was most desolate : the hackney-coaches, with four horses strolling about like ghosts, the foot-passengers few but the lowest of the people.

Sir Walter Scott, 1771-1832

In February o' a favoured year,
Nae puddock suld croot nor croon,
But rampin' showers o' hail and sleet,
Come rakin' o'er the moon.

Traditional

from From the Border Hills

All day on the first of February the snow fell. The morning mail from Dumfries did not reach Moffat on its way to Edinburgh until late in the afternoon, and it seemed sheer madness to go on, with the terrible five miles up to the Beef Tub to be faced, and after that the long stretch over the hills to Tweedsmuir, where drifts were bound to be deep. But MacGeorge, the guard, an old soldier, 'stern and not given to speak', was determined to make the attempt to get the mails through... So, in a rising gale and blinding snow, the coach crawled away from the inn up Moffat High Street. Three dreadful miles were travelled, slowly and more slowly, until the coach stuck fast in a drift from which no effort of the straining team, reinforced by the extra horses used in bad weather for the long pull out of Moffat, could drag it. Again the guard was begged to turn now and go back; again he refused. The horses were taken out; some were sent back to Moffat with the stable-lads in charge of the extra tracers, and two, loaded with the mail-bags, were led on by Goodfellow, the coachman, and the guard. The Moffat roadman, Marchbanks, who had been a passenger in the coach, went with them, and they battled on towards Tweedshaws, four miles ahead. After half that distance the horses could not be urged any further.

'What say ye, Jamie ?' said coachman to guard.

'Come ye or bide ye, I *gang on,*' was MacGeorge's answer, and to that the coachman responded, 'If ye gang, I gang.'

The horses were turned loose to make the best they could of it, Marchbanks was persuaded to try to return to Moffat, and together, carrying the mails, those two faithful servants, the guard and coachman, plodded away into the snow and the dark. They were never seen alive again.

By the following morning the storm had died down, and the whole countryside lay shrouded deep in drifts in that brooding frightening hush that succeeds a blizzard. The snow-posts were covered almost to their tops when Marchbanks, anxious to discover the fate of MacGeorge and Goodfellow, toiled up the steep ascent again. He found the abandoned coach, a great white mound, and far beyond the place where he had turned back on the previous night he saw, hanging to a snow-post, the mail-bags, securely fastened there by bleeding hands. Of the two men there was no sign...

...They were found at last, on an old disused pack or drove road – some say the searchers were guided to it by a dream – days after they had set out, not far from each other, lying quietly as if asleep. A shepherd who saw them said that on MacGeorge's dead face, so stern in life, was 'a kind o' pleesure'.

Molly Clavering, 1900-1995

The bard of the clan MacGregor is laid to rest, 30 October 1932. Ray Topping, Alasdair Alpin MacGregor Collection, SEA

from A gravestone in Moffat Kirkyard

Sacred to the memory of James McGeorge Guard of the Dumfries and Edinburgh Royal Mail who unfortunately perished at the age of 47 near Tweedshaws after the most strenuous exertions in the performance of his duty during that memorable snow storm 1st February 1831.

from The Gowk Storm

GOWK STORM. A storm of several days at the end at the end of April or the beginning of May ; an evil or abstract obstruction of short duration.

'Wrap yoursels up weel,' Nannie told Julia and me, 'for I can tell frae the feel in the wind that it's the Gowk Storm that's boding.'

We were standing in the kitchen before setting off for Barnfingal. Nannie's face was fire-flushed as she stooped over the girdle. It was not her usual baking-day, but Mr Ferguson, the Balmader minister, had come to visit papa, and visitors were as important to Nannie as they were to us. I asked her to give me something to eat before I left and she lifted from the girdle, with hands dusted with flour, a pancake which was so gloriously hot I had to keep changing it from hand to hand as I ate it.

'There is something so unlikely about snow in April,' Julia said pensively, staring out of the little side window.

'Ay,' Nannie conceded, 'juist when the farmers are talking o'sowing and lambing. But it's the unlikely things that always happen in this world.'

'The poor lambs and primroses,' condoled Julia.

'It will pass if they but thole it,' Nannie said summarily, sitting on the creepie with the bellows between her knees and blowing the fire brighter. 'That's whit Gowk Storm means, something o' ill-chance that micht fa' to ony o' us and that willna bide.'

Nancy Brysson Morrison, 1907-1986

from *Statistical Account of Scotland 1793*

Curling is a favourite diversion among the commonalty: and even the gentlemen sometimes join in it.

Rev William Miller of Crawfordjohn, 1719-1801

Their chief amusement in winter is curling, or playing stones on smooth ice: they eagerly vie with one another who shall come nearest the mark, and one part of the parish against another, one description of men against another, one trade or occupation against another, and often one whole parish against another – earnestly contending for the 'palm' which is generally all the prize; except perhaps the victors claim from the vanquished, the dinner, and bowl of toddy which, to do them justice, both commonly take together with great cordiality, and generally without any grudge at the fortune of the day, or remembrance of their late combat with one another, wisely reflecting no doubt that defeat as well as victory is the fate of war. Those accustomed to this amusement or that have acquired dexterity at the game are extremely fond of it. The amusement itself is healthy: it is innocent: it does nobody harm: let them enjoy it.

Rev John Sheppard of Muirkirk, 1741-1799

Winter sports on Duddingston Loch. Charles Altamont Doyle

DANGEROUS.

1981's was a savage winter. Snow lay eighteen inches deep in Kelvingrove Park. Miss Caldwell in layers of outdated woollens huddled over a one-bar electric fire in her cavernous first-floor sitting-room. Listening to the radio in her gaunt damp flat, Miss McLeod was almost sure she heard the announcer say the name of her teacher-friend who'd returned to Aberdeenshire when he read out a news item about a woman having been snowed in and dying in a black-out. With this terrible new sadness to bear and no way of confirming it (the newsagent's was at the world's end), she lost much of her own will to live this winter out. Through the icy windows Huntly Gardens was like an arctic wilderness, beyond saving. A pipe had burst in the kitchen, now another split in the bathroom; the gas went funny and wouldn't light, she ran out of matches to try; the radio battery faded to nothing, and she retired without hope to bed, her head humming with memories. She'd exhausted the supplies of food in her larder, was too proud to use her phone to summon help and died of pneumonia and starvation in the course of three long days and nights when the snows blown from Greenland blizzarded across Glasgow's genteel West End and transformed it into a frozenly beautiful winter composition by Sisley or Pissarro.

Ronald Frame, b1953

Snow on the Meadows, Edinburgh. Dave Reed

from *Ille Terrarum*

But noo the auld city, street by street,
An' winter fu' o' snaw an' sleet
A while shut in my gangrel feet
    An' goavin' mettle;
Noo is the soopit ingle sweet,
     An' liltin' kettle.

An' noo the winter winds complain;
Cauld lies the glaur in ilka lane;
On draigled hizzie, tautit wean
    An' drucken lads,
In the mirk nicht, the winter rain
    Dribbles an' blads.

Whan bugles frae the Castle rock,
An' beaten drums wi' dowie shock,
Wauken, at cauld-rife sax o'clock,
    My chitterin' frame,
I mind me on the kintry cock,
    The kintry hame.

I mind me on yon bonny bield;
An' Fancy traivels far afield
To gaither a' that gairdens yield
    O' sun an' Simmer;
To hearten up a dowie chield,
    Fancy's the limmer!

Robert Louis Stevenson, 1850-1894

from *Deskford Parish*

Being born in a crofter's cottage in Deskford in north-east Scotland on a cold December day in 1924 life was a lottery. Infant deaths were normal then. The first, third and sixth-born of our family of nine all died in infancy. I was the eighth-born of our family.

Six-feet (2m)-deep snowdrifts were not uncommon. In 1947 we were snowed-in to an extent I had not seen before and after digging our way out we walked on top of the snow and actually had to bend down to touch the telephone wires, so deep were the drifts. In winter we kept a shovel behind the door to dig our way to the well across the road.

Occasionally, roads would be blocked for two or three weeks by which time the two shops in Berryhillock village would have run out of groceries. My late Uncle, Jimmy Muiry, a tailor turned grocer with petrol-pump, who owned and had run the shop at the top of the village since 1923, would organise a trip by horse-sledge to Cullen some four miles away for emergency supplies of groceries.

Farm houses in the 1930s did not have central heating nor wall-to-wall carpeting. Our living-room comprised 4ft(1.3m) square flagstones of slate some of which acted as a barometer to advise impending rain by exuding damp. The only floor covering was a clippy-mat in front of the expansive fireplace with its ingle nooks and huge cast-iron kettle hung high on the sway. The peat fire was hot enough to burn our bare legs tartan while our backs felt like blocks of ice.

George Anderson Clarke, b1924

When Tintoc tap puts on his cap,
And Culter on his cowl,
The wise auld wives o' Symington
Cry out it will be foul.

Traditional

Cottages near Fort William.

from Sir Patrick Spens

They hadna sail'd a league, a league,
A league but barely three,
When the lift grew dark, and the wind blew loud,
And gurly grew the sea.

The ankers brak, and the topmasts lap,
It was sic a deadly storm,
And the waves cam oer the broken ship,
Till a' her sides were torn.

'O where will I get a gude sailor,
To take my helm in hand,
Till I get up to the tall topmast,
To see if I can spy land?'

'O here am I, a sailor gude,
To take the helm in hand,
Till you go up to the tall topmast;
But I fear you'll neer spy land.'

He hadna gane a step, a step,
A step but barely ane,
When a bout flew out of our goodly ship,
And the salt sea it came in.

* * *

O laith, laith were our gude Scots lords
To weet their cork-heeled shoon!
But lang or a' the play was play'd,
They wat their hats aboon.

And mony was the feather bed
That flatter'd on the faem,
And mony was the gude lord's son
That never mair cam hame.

The ladyes wrang their fingers white,
The maidens tore their hair,

A' for the sake of their true loves;
For them they'll see nae mair.

*　*　*

Half-owre, half-owre to Aberdour,
'Tis fifty fathoms deep,
And there lies gude Sir Patrick Spens,
Wi the Scots lords at his feet.

Traditional

from Witchcraft and Superstitious Record in the South-western District of Scotland

With the history of the South-western district of Scotland the life story of Sir Robert Grierson of Lag, or 'Aul' Lag' ... is intimately associated ...

The year of grace, 1733, was wearing fast towards Yule, when one stormy night a small vessel found herself overtaken, at the mouth of the Solway, by a gale of wind that was almost too much for her. Close-hauled and fighting for every foot of sea-way she was slowly forcing her way up-channel against the angry north-west blast when a strange adventure befell her. In a lull following a savage squall the moon broke through the black flying cloud, lighting up the storm-tossed sea and revealing to those aboard another struggling sail far astern. Curiously the sea-men gazed, but searching glance gave way to wonder, and wonder to fear, when they saw what had at first seemed a craft like themselves, come rushing onwards in the very teeth of the wind, and with as much ease as if running 'free' before it. The moon dipped, and again darkness descended on the face of the waters, but not for long. Once again the moonlight pierced the curtain of flying cloud. Then was seen what surely was the strangest craft that ever sailed the tossing Solway sea – a great State-coach, drawn by six jet-black horses, with out-riders, coachmen, and a great retinue of torch bearers, footmen, and followers, furiously driving onwards over the foam-crested waves. As the phantom carriage plunged nearer, the skipper, regaining some little of his courage, ran forwards, hailing in sailor fashion -'Where bound? and where from?' – the answer came back, clear and distinct across the raging waters – 'to tryst with Lag ! Dumfries: from Hell !'

J Maxwell Wood, 1868-1925

"OH! WERT THOU IN THE CAULD BLAST."

O, Wert Thou in the Cauld Blast

O wert thou in the cauld blast
On yonder lea, on yonder lea,
My plaidie to the angry airt,
I'd shelter thee, I'd shelter thee.
Or did Misfortune's bitter storms
Around thee blaw, around thee blaw,
Thy bield should be my bosom,
To share it a', to share it a'.

Or were I in the wildest waste,
Sae black and bare, sae black and bare,
The desert were a Paradise,
If thou wert there, if thou wert there,
Or were I monarch of the globe,
Wi' thee to reign, wi' thee to reign,
The brightest jewel in my crown
Wad be my queen, wad be my queen.

Robert Burns, 1759-1796

from Visiting Staffa with Mendelssohn

9 August 1829

On the said early morning, the agreeable steam-persons, who at first came flying towards us with nothing but olive-leaves, became lower and lower the more the barometer sank and the sea rose. For that the Atlantic did. It stretched its thousand feelers more and more roughly, twirling us about like anything. The ship household kept its breakfast almost for itself, few people aboard being able to manage their cups and saucers. Ladies, as a rule, fell down like flies, and one of the other gentlemen followed their example.

I only wish my travelling fellow-sufferer had not been among them, but he is on better terms with the sea as a musician than as an individual or a stomach.

Two beautiful cold daughters of a Hebrides aristocrat, at whom Felix may storm, quietly continued sitting on deck, and did not even care much for the seasickness of their own mother. Also, there sat placidly by the steam engine, warming herself in the cold wind, a woman of two-and-eighty. That woman has six times touched me, and seven times irritated me. She wanted to see Staffa before her end. Staffa, with its strange basalt pillars and caverns, is in all picture-books.

We were put in boats and lifted by the hissing sea up the pillar stumps to the celebrated Fingal's Cave. A greener roar of waves surely never rushed into a stranger cavern – its many pillars making it look like the inside of an immense organ, black and resounding, absolutely without purpose, and quite alone, the wide grey sea within and without. There the old woman scrambled about laboriously, close to the water. She wanted to see the cave of Staffa before her end; and she saw it.

We returned in the little boat to our steamer, to that unpleasant steam smell. When the second boat arrived, I could see with what truth at the theatre they represent the rising and falling of a boat, when the hero saves the heroine out of some trouble. There was a certain comfort in seeing that the two aristocratic faces had, after all, turned pale as I looked at them through my black eye-glass. The two-and-eighty-years old woman was also in the boat, trembling. The boat went up and down. With difficulty she was lifted out – but she had seen Staffa before her end.

Karl Klingemann, 1798-1862

Fingal's Cave, Staffa.

from The Journal of a Tour to the Hebrides
with Samuel Johnson

Crossing from Skye to Coll Sunday 3 October 1773

Joseph reported that the wind was still against us. Dr Johnson said, 'A wind, or not a wind? that is the question'; for he can amuse himself at times with a little play of words, or rather sentences.

Our vessel often lay so much on one side, that I trembled lest she should be overset, and indeed they told me afterwards, that they had run her sometimes to within an inch of the water, so anxious were they to make what waste they could before the night should be worse. I now saw what I have never saw before, a prodigious sea, with immense billows coming upon a vessel, so as that it seemed hardly possible to escape. There was something grandly horrible in the sight. I am glad I have seen it once. Amidst all these terrifying circumstances, I endeavoured to compose my mind. It was not easy to do it; for all the stories that I had heard of the dangerous sailing among the Hebrides, which is proverbial, came full upon my recollection. When I thought of those who were dearest to me, and would suffer severely, should I be lost, I upbraided myself, as not having a sufficient cause for putting myself in such danger.

It was half an hour after eleven before we set ourselves in the course for Col. As I saw them all busy doing something, I asked Col, with much earnestness,

Samuel Johnson and James Boswell touring the Hebrides.

what I could do. He, with a happy readiness, put into my hand a rope, which was fixed to the top of one of the masts, and told me to hold it till he bade me pull. If I had considered the matter, I might have seen that this could not be of the least service ; but his object was to keep me out of the way of those who were busy working the vessel, and at the same time to divert my fear, by employing me, and making me think that I was of use. Thus did I stand firm to my post, while the wind and rain beat upon me, always expecting a call to pull my rope.

Dr Johnson had all this time been quiet and unconcerned. He had lain down on one of the beds, and having got free from sickness, was satisfied. The truth is, he knew nothing of the danger we were in ; but, fearless and unconcerned, might have said, in the words which he had chosen for the motto to his *Rambler,*

Quo me cunque rapit tempestas, deferor hospes

For as the tempest drives, I shape my way.

James Boswell, 1740-1795

from *A letter to Mrs Thrale 1773*

From the autumnal to the vernal equinox a dry day is hardly known, except when the showers are suspended by a tempest.

Samuel Johnson 1709-1784

A wind-bent tree, Lismore.
Alasdair Alpin MacGregor
Collection, SEA

A strong north-east wind came howling down the empty streets. The lamps were just lit, sending wavering reflections into the pools of water left by the recent rain. Every now and then came a gust of wind that blew Alex's dress against her ankles, and nearly buffeted her hat off.

Coming straight out of the overheated room, the cold was at first almost refreshing, but before she had gone more than a very little way, she was conscious of an overpowering weariness.

She stood for a moment on the wet pavement, whilst the wind drove her petticoats in flapping wreaths about her ankles; it beat her umbrella until she had to put it down, and as she came to the bridge she stopped for a little to readjust her hat and breathe, before beginning to struggle across the unprotected bit of roadway.

Her excitement had all died down now. She felt more than ever sure that she had failed, that the whole thing had fallen quite flat, and that she had only made an exhibition of herself – all for five pounds! Why could she not have just stayed at home and scrimped upon something else, instead of supposing that her pitiful scrap of talent could astonish the public and make money? Were there not actors by the score – people of real genius, and thoroughly trained in their art – who could barely make a living, and she – she!

In her pitiful self-depreciation her heart sank to her very boots. Oh, she was tired! It was a dismal evening, and a dismal world at times, but what was the use of grumbling? She had got to sludge back to the station in the rain, and then go home and give a cheerful account of her day, that would make the others feel it had been quite a success. Alex was halfway across the bridge by this time, and a moment's lull in the wind made her stop again, to gather up her skirts better out of the mud.

'I'll never wear a long skirt out of vanity again,' she thought. 'It hasn't really made much difference to my appearance, and it only makes me look silly in the street, and doubles the bother of walking.'

She stood looking down for a moment across the parapet of the bridge, held, as always by the beauty of a scene that even the remorseless climate could not destroy. On either side of the blue gulf, high houses shone with lighted windows; in the yellow and stormy sky, great masses of vapour rolled above the town, and parted to a clearer space in the east. A darker point pricked out here and there from the mists, and far down below between its gardened banks, the water ran like a ravelled white thread.

'Oh, I'm so cold!' thought Alex, turning again with a shiver – remembering with a woman's envy, the only face amongst her audience that she had readily noticed: a woman rather older than herself, with the smooth flesh spread perhaps too thickly on cheeks that glowed with health and self-delight. Alex had noticed the poise of her shoulders and the fur cloak lined with white satin that hung across the chair. 'Dress like that would make any one look handsome!' she thought, with another bitter shiver. 'Oh, there is the rain on again, and, my good hat! – I must put up my umbrella! Never, never again, as long as I live, shall I wear a hat that spoils with rain!'

Now, you must understand that when Alex put up her umbrella she had to let go of her long skirt that went slopping down on one side, and she could no longer hold on her hat, which was immediately nearly blown off by the wind.

Jane and Mary Findlater, 1866-1946, 1865-1963

The Reid in the Loch Sayis

Thocht raging storms movis us to schaik,
And wind makis waters us ouerflow,
We yeild thairto bot dois not brek,
And in the calme bent up we grow.

So baneist men, thocht prices raige,
And prisoners be not disparit,
Abyde the calm quhill that it suaige;
For tyme sic caussis hes reparit.

Traditional

from Skye : the Island and its Legends

My father and I were at Kingsburgh at the time of King George V's long illness. About two miles away, up the hill, lived an old man of over eighty ; he had been a stalker and had been one of those present when King George, as a boy, had shot his first stag. He was intensely anxious, as was the whole island, for news of the King. Every night, in the black dark – for it was a wet and cloudy winter – he walked down to us for news, and every night the news seemed less hopeful. Then came the great storm, one of the worst I have seen in the Hebrides : all night long the house shook and thunder growled. After breakfast my father and his setter Nora went out to look at the weather, and Nora was lifted off her feet and blown across the lawn: I never saw so frightened a dog. Throughout the day the storm raged and snow fell in heavy squally showers, but by evening the wind began to drop a little. Our usual visitor arrived. This time he did not ask 'How is my King?' but 'Is my King still alive? We said that he was, but that there was still no change or improvement. 'He will do now,' said the old man.

Rough weather in the Sound of Mull.

Next night, to our surprise, he did not come, but a slight improvement in the King's condition was reported. When the next day again passed without a visit we feared the walk through the storm had been too much for his heart, never very good, and went up to inquire and to bring him the latest (and good) news of his King. We found him busy on his croft and gave him the news. 'Ay, my King will do now,' he said again. Then we asked why he had suddenly stopped his visits of inquiry and he replied quite simply: 'That was a Royal storm. It came for my King, but he did not go with it. When a Royal storm is sent back empty, my mother told me, the one for whom it came would live and do well. I never saw a Royal storm sent back before.' We asked him if he had ever seen a Royal storm before, and did they only come for the soul of a king? No, he said, any great man, and not every king, only the great. He himself had seen the one that came for Lord Kitchener, but Kitchener went with it. 'It is seldom that a Royal storm is sent back. But my King is a very great man.'

Otta F Swire, 1898-1973

<i>from</i> A Voyage Round the Coasts of Scotland and the Isles

Colonsay, 30 June 1841

All pleasant passages in human life conclude at last. We heard the rattling of the blast without as it rushed from tree to chimney, to show its impartial character, or howled past doors and windows, like a hungry wolf seeking what it might devour. Withstanding all entreaties to remain for the night beneath the shelter of that kindly roof, we concluded with a small deoch-an-doruis from an ancient quaich, and bidding farewell to our hospitable friends, we buckled on our pea-jackets, drew our south-westers over our brows, tried to look grim and bold, and then sallied forth, having the same three miles or thereby to take us to the Cutter as had brought us hither, with little chance of their proving much shorter in darkness than in daylight. The rain drove against us all the way like split peas, and the aforesaid road (now by courtesy so called), which was well enough in the morning in its own wild way, had by this time been converted in many places to something like a muddy river. Our own clay assuredly was moist enough before we got on board, but it is a sustaining thought to know that one is serving their Queen and country, and we ourself never cared much for rain-water at any time; so, after looking a little at the cabin fire (which was bright and beautiful) and also at a red herring and a glass of ale, merely to encourage commerce, we retired to our respective places of repose.

James Wilson, 1795-1856

from Mark Chapter IV in The New Testament in Scots

Detail from a shell cup.
Phoebe Traquair

The same day, whan eenin cam on, he said til them, 'Lat's atowre tae the the tither side o the Loch.' Sae they skailed the thrang an tuik him wi them i the boat whaur he was sittin; an the' war ither boats wi him forbye.

Belyve a fell wind begoud tae blaw, an the jaws jaupit intil the boat, till it wis naur at the sinkin. Meantime Jesus was lyin asleep i the stern wi his heid on the coad. They waukent him, cryin til him, 'Maister, carena-ye by, an us like tae be drouned?'

Sae he rase an shored the wind an caa'd tae the waves, 'Wheesht ye, be quait'; an the wind dilled doun, an aa wis lown an caum. Syne he said til them, 'What maks ye sic cuifs? Hae ye ey nae faith?' An they war fell feared an said til ither, 'Wha can this be, at een wind an wave dis his biddin?'

translated by William Lorimer, 1885-1967

in A letter from a St Kilda mailboat washed up in September 1885

I beg leave to intimate to you that I am directed by the people under my charge on this island to tell you that their corn, barley, and potatoes are destroyed by a great storm which passed over the island on Saturday and Sabbath last. You will be kind enough to apply to Government in order to send us a supply of corn seed, barley and potatoes. This year's crop is quite useless. They never before saw such a storm at this time of the year. They have lost one of their boats; but happily there was no loss of life.

Rev John Mackay, c1805-1901

Is balbh gach sian ach a' ghaoth.
Dumb is all weather but the wind.

Gaelic proverb

Merch said tae Aperill,
I saw three hoggs on yonder hill,
An if ye'll lend me dayis three,
I'll find a wey tae gar them dee.
The first o' them was wind an weet,
The neist o' them was snaw an sleet,
The third o' them was sic a freeze,
It friz the birds' nebs till the trees ;
An whan the three days were past an gane,
The silly puir hoggies cam hirplin hame.

Traditional

Sheep sheltering from the wind, Stones of Stenness, Orkney. Dave Reed

from No Oxbridge Spires

I've never been able to push a pram straight which is probably something to do with the fact that once I was able to fly. Well of course it's a well known fact that black people could fly before slavery days and that our wings are reforming was rather more perambulatory. There I was in my pram only a few months old. As I was four pounds at birth I don't reckon that I weighed more than a half dozen bags of sugar at the time. Anyway, it was a windy day and my mum and auntie wanted to go to a drapers shop along at Crown Street in the Gorbals. Well as I said it was windy and my granddad said, 'Don't you be taking my precious out in that weather.' Well, my mum and my auntie persisted, so there we all were setting out on 'The Curtain Mission' with my big cousin Linda, or was it Yvonne, who was only six at the time.

Well, you wouldn't think that between them my mum and my auntie had brought up four children because weren't they daft enough to put up the hood so that I wouldn't be in a draft. So there we were half way along Caledonia Road when Whoosh! Off I fly like the ancestors on my daddy's side. Over the railings, into the park, which dear reader I feel obliged to point out was only yards from the Clyde. My mum rushed into the park and found me still strapped in and, so the story goes, smiling sweetly. My auntie on the other hand had to go to hospital to get stitches because she held onto the pram when it took flight and was impaled on the railings and my cousin lost a couple of milkteeth.

Maud Sulter, b1960

Cold Wind in May

There's nothing more to say to this North wind.
The buds peer from the entrances of their burrows
And come no further out, and the tortured thrush
Swings in delirium in its cage of branches.

It's all been said already. March and April
Held up their terms of truce deckled with all
Their youngest, tenderest flowers. But they're torn up
And whirled into space above the factory wall.

We still find fragments blown beneath the hedges.
Or, at some corner, at his cafe table
The sun lifts up his lazy glass of wine,
Says something charming, smiles for being fickle.

Be careful, passer-by. Where you are walking
Summer will scrawl its long nostalgia over
The panting stones and open gardens out
In drugged and dizzy manuscripts of flowers.

You'll read no stories of the North wind.
Buds will have perished, thrush escaped from his song.
But you'll be singing still in your leafless branches
High in the dark, your year forever young.

Norman MacCaig, b1910

from Scotland

This is my country,
The land that begat me,
These windy spaces
Are surely my own.

Sir Alexander Gray, 1882-1968

from *Tam o' Shanter*

The wind blew as 'twad blawn its last;
The rattling showers rose on the blast;
The speedy gleams the darkness swallow'd;
Loud, deep, and lang the thunder bellow'd:
That night, a child might understand,
The Deil had business on his hand.

Weel mounted on his gray mare, Meg,
A better never lifted leg,
Tam skelpit on thro' dub and mire,
Despising wind, and rain, and fire;
Whiles holding fast, his guid blue bonnet,
Whiles crooning o'er some auld Scots sonnet.;
Whiles glow'ring round wi' prudent cares,
Lest bogles catch him unawares:
Kirk-Alloway was drawing nigh,
Where ghaists and houlets nightly cry.

Robert Burns, 1759-1796

Tam o'Shanter pursued by the witch Nannie.

O! Are Ye Sleepin, Maggie?

'O! Are ye sleepin, Maggie?
   O! are ye sleepin, Maggie?
Let me in, for loud the linn
   Is roarin o'er the warlock craigie!

'Mirk an rainy is the nicht,
   No a starn in a the carry;
Lightnin's gleam athwart the lift,
   An win's drive wi winter's fury.

'Fearfu' soughs the boor-tree bank,
   The rifted wood roars wild an dreary,
Loud the iron yett does clank,
   The cry o howlets mak's me eerie.

'Aboon my breath I daurna speak,
   For fear I rouse your waukrif daddie.
Caul's the blast upon my cheek, –
   O rise, rise my bonnie ladie!'

She oped the door, she loot him in:
   He cuist aside his dreepin plaidie:
'Blaw your warst, ye rain an win,
   Since, Maggie, now I'm in aside ye.

Robert Tannahill, 1774-1810

An uair a laidheas a' ghaoth, 's maoth gach sian.
No weather's ill if the wind be still.

Gaelic proverb

from *Folklore 1885*

It is a common saying among the Rosehearty fisherfolks that marriages amongst them bring stormy weather. A very common season for marrying is immediately after the herring fishing is finished.

WEATHER REPORTS. ILLUSTRATED. "A Gael Blowing!"

P.V.B

from The Speak of the Mearns

Father turned round 'Not cold are you then,' and you said you weren't, neither you were, just frozen in a wonder looking at the sky, arching and rising in the coming night. What if God made a bit slip some time and cracked the sky and came tumbling through, box of spunks still gripped in his hand and splashing the water so high from the sea it went pelting high up across the Howe –

And then you were feared, you held your breath, tight, there was the crack, growing wider and wider, a splurge on the lift, the dark behind, light in front, the splurge blue and yellow, the gulls had stopped that daft crying and crying and the wind had stilled, why didn't father see, He was coming, He was coming.

Boom!

Something flickered from the crack, and father raised his head.

' 'Od, we'll need to be holding back. There's the thunder, Keith, it'll frighten your Mother.'

That thunder-pelt was the beginning of the wettest Spring that had come on the Howe for many a day, all that night it thundered and rained, in turn, when one had finished with splitting the sky and scarting its claws along the earth and over through the dripping parks, the other came down in blinding pelts, the swash of it warping through roofs and walls, the cattle court of Balhaggarty was flooded out and half the stock drowned, at Moss Bank Sandy the dafty had come home gey late from a boozing ploy and gone into the smiddy where the coals still glowed and sat him down for a bit of a warm before sneaking up the stairs to his bed. And faith if he didn't fall fast asleep and was woke with a smack of cold water in his face, the smiddy swirling with a thing like a wave, he thought between the coals and the water he was surely in hell at last.

Lewis Grassic Gibbon, 1901-1935

from The Seasons

Then comes the father of the tempest forth,
Wrapt in black glooms. First, joyless rains obscure
Drive through the mingling skies with vapour foul,
Dash on the mountain's brow, and shake the woods
That grumbling wave below. The unsightly plain
Lies a brown deluge; as the low-bent clouds
Pour flood on flood, yet unexhausted still
Combine, and, deepening into night, shut up
The day's fair face. The wanderers of heaven,
Each to his home, retire; save those that love
To take their pastime in the troubled air,
Or skimming flutter round the dimply pool.
The cattle from the untasted fields return,
And ask, with meaning low, their wonted stalls,
Or ruminate in the contiguous shade.
Thither the household feathery people crowd -
The crested cock, with all his female train,
Pensive and ripping; while the cottage hind
Hangs o'er the enlivening blaze, and taleful there,
Recounts his simple frolic; much he talks,
And much he laughs, nor recks the storm that blows
Without, and rattles on his humble roof.
Wide o'er the brim, with many a torrent swelled,
And the mixed ruin of its banks o'erspread,
At last the roused-up river pours along:
Resistless, roaring, dreadful, down it comes,
From the rude mountain and the mossy wild,
Tumbling through rocks abrupt, and sounding far;
Then o'er the sanded valley floating spreads,
Calm, sluggish silent; till again, constrained
Between two meeting hills, it bursts a way
Where rocks and woods o'erhang the turbid stream;
There, gathering triple force, rapid and deep,
It boils, and wheels, and foams, and thunders through.

James Thomson, 1700-1748

[53]

from *The Journal of Queen Victoria*

Holyrood, 25 August 1881

A bright morning, to my joy, on waking. By the time we were at breakfast, the sky clouded over, but there was wind and we all hoped it looked as if it might keep fine ... There was a little rain, but it cleared off again. Affie and Marie came to luncheon, and by that time the rain increased, and behold, whilst I was dressing, down it came! There was a perfect sea of umbrellas. The sky became white and

Queen Victoria's review of Scottish Volunteers at Edinburgh: view from St Anthony's Chapel.
Illustrated London News 3 September 1881

grey, with mist in the distance, and the ground where the march past was to take place, which could be seen from the windows, and which had partially recovered from yesterday's rain, became like a lake of muddy water, too distressing.

There was nothing for it, but to start with waterproofs and umbrellas; but the gentlemen and servants, and all the poor volunteers, had to remain without any of these protections. We started at quarter to 4, in the open landau and four, Beatrice and Marie sitting opposite to me, Affie, Arthur, George C. and his staff,

and my gentlemen, all in uniform, riding with us. As we came out of the court-yard, we first turned to the right and inspected the cavalry, which extended some way up the Queen's Drive, then turned round again, and proceeded right down the line, to the saluting point, behind which was a large stand full of spectators. In the enclosure, below it, stood the unfortunate Archers' Guard, who were drenched, and looked very cold, the Duke of Abercorn being at their head. The marching past then began, in a sea of mud, most despairing to witness. There was 40,000 men, and such fine ones ... Once or twice it seemed as though the rain were going to cease, but only to come down again with renewed force. Pitilessly it came down, drifted by a high wind, on all those poor men, who nevertheless continued marching steadily along, with patient and gallant endurance. How different to the Review, 21 years ago, in bright sunshine, when dearest Mama went with me, and dearest Albert rode by my side!

At 6 we got back, coming in through the garden, and scrambled into the house by a lower passage, close to the kitchen, everyone soaked, but I only partially so, down the side from which the wind came, and while I sat in a pool of water. I had to change many under-garments.

Queen Victoria, 1819-1901

from *The Eglinton Tournament and Gentleman Unmasked*

Eglinton Tournament, 29 August 1839

This should have been the second day of the Tournament; but the morning was ushered in by storm, and doubt and anxiety pervaded the minds of thousands. Bitter as the rain was, and wild the wind, numerous parties hied them to Eglinton as a charmed spot. Hundreds of visitors, too, who had been unable to attend on the first day, came in from a distance, in spite of wind and weather, and amongst these were numerous deputations from Edinburgh, Glasgow, Dumfries, &c. At an early hour, a rumour got abroad that the work of the Tournament would be entirely give up, from the bitterness of the weather, and this impression was afterwards officially confirmed, by an intimation from Lord Eglinton, to the regret of thousands, though all at the same time felt pain that his lordship was likely to be baulked by the elements in giving a national treat, which the present generation may not witness again. If the strangers could not see the tilting, they resolved to see the tilting ground, and during the forenoon, the grounds and lists were covered by some thousands, who feasted their eyes, and expressed the hope that a change of weather might yet allow the tourney to be enacted in proper style.

Though all regretted the event, as we have said, no one could affix blame; and the result showed, that causes to which all human intentions and actions sink into abject insignificance, had alone, for a time, clouded the expectations of the mass; for the wish to gratify was prominent in every action of the lord of the Tournament. About mid-day the clouds dispersed, and the sun showed his welcome countenance; thousands, who had till then kept their chambers, were invited out, and at two o'clock the grounds of Eglinton were nearly as much crowded as before.

Peter Buchan, 1790-1854

from *A letter to Disraeli*

29 August 1839

I must write you a line of thanks for remembering me at such a moment. You tell me to send you accounts of the Tournament which, alas! has been spoiled by the weather. Nothing could have been more perfect than all the arrangements. The lists all beautiful and most picturesque with all the tents and encampments. The procession was gorgeous and the whole reception splendid, 300 feet of temporary room having been erected, thousands and thousands flocking from everywhere, even from America when as usual in our horrible climate down came that sort of vicious, spiteful pour that never visits other countries except in the rainy season when people know what to expect and make their arrangements accordingly.

My Ist feeling was to sit down and cry.

Lady Londonderry, 1800-1865

For a while he swaggered round the empty platform and smoked a cigarette. Milk-cans clanked in a shed mournfully. Gourlay had a congenital horror of eerie sounds – he was his mother's son for that – and he fled to the waiting room, to avoid the hollow clang. It was a June afternoon, of brooding heat, and a band of yellow sunshine was lying on the glazed table, showing every scratch in its surface. The place oppressed him ; he was sorry he had come. But he plunged into his novel and forgot the world.

He started in fear when a voice addressed him. He looked up, and here it was only the baker – the baker with his reddish fringe of beard and his honest grin, which wrinkled up his face to his eyes in merry and kindly wrinkles. He had a wonderful hearty manner with a boy.

'Ay man, John, it's you,' said the baker. 'Dod, I'm just in time. The storm's at the burstin' !'

'Storm!' said Gourlay. He had a horror of lightning since the day of his birth.

'Aye, we're in for a pelter. What have you been doing that you didna see't?'

They went to the window. The fronting heavens were a black purple. The thunder, which had been growling in the distance, swept forward and roared above the town. The crash no longer rolled afar, but cracked close to the ear, hard, crepitant. Quick lightning stabbed the world in vicious and repeated hate. A blue-black moistness lay heavy on the cowering earth. The rain came – a few drops at first, sullen, as if loath to come, that splashed on the pavement wide as a crown piece ; then a white rush of slanting spears. A great blob shot in through the window, open at the top, and spat wide on Gourlay's cheek. It was lukewarm. He started violently – that warmth on his cheek brought the terror so near.

The heavens were rent with a crash, and the earth seemed on fire. Gourlay screamed in terror.

The baker put his arm round him in kindly protection.

'Tuts, man, dinna be feared,' he said. 'You're John Gourlay's son, ye know. You ought to be a hardy man.'

'Ay, but I'm no,' chattered John, the truth coming out in his fear. 'I just let on to be.'

But the worst was soon over. Lightning, both sheeted and forked, was vivid as ever, but the thunder slunk growling away.

'The heavens are opening and shutting like a man's eye,' said Gourlay. 'Oh, it's a terrible thing the world !' and he covered his face with his hands.

A flash shot into a mounded wood far away. 'It stabbed it like a dagger!' stared Gourlay.

'Look, look, did ye see yon ? It came down in a broad flash – then jerked to the side – then ran down to a sharp point again. It was like the coulter of a plough.'

Suddenly a blaze of lightning flamed wide, and a fork shot down its centre.

'That,' said Gourlay, 'was like a red crack in a white-hot furnace door.'

'Man, you're a noticing boy,' said the baker.

George Douglas Brown, 1869-1902

from Stormy Weather

Since the minister was also a trustee of the orphanage, his requests were almost impossible to deny. Matron had conceded, 'allowing' the girls to attend the Band of Hope. But with one proviso – depending on the weather!

It was this proviso that kept Chris glued to her position in front of the window, searching for signs in the morning sky. For it didn't need rain itself to cancel the weekly outing. The 'threat' of rain was enough for Matron to defy the minister, and the whole United Free Kirk of Scotland.

Oh! Never had a small girl of fourteen been up against such a powerful adversary. And never was an autumn and winter so full of Fridays which 'threatened rain'! Nor even more the runes of childhood so fervently invoked could diminish the threat :

> Rainie, rainie rattlestanes
> dinna rain on me
> rain on Johnnie Groat's hoose
> far across the sea ...

Preaching on the shore, Skye.

Second bell clanging through the dormitory stirred the sleepers into disgruntled wakefulness, and filled the room with complaint. Alice, unaware at last of Chris keeping vigil, and of the reason for such a vigil, shuffled towards the window.

'It's going to rain,' she prophesied. 'It's going to pour! We won't get to the Band of Hope tonight.'

Jessie Kesson, 1915-1994

from Captain Malcolm MacLeod's account in 'The Lyon in Mourning'

Prince Charles Edward Stuart arriving on Skye, 2 July 1746

About 7 o'clock at night he went on board the above mentioned small boat ... They had not well left the shore till the wind blew a hard gale, and the sea became so very rough and tempestuous that all on board begged he would return; for the waves were beating over and over them, the men tugging hard at the oars, and Captain MacLeod laving the water out of the little boat. The Prince would by no means hear of returning, and to divert the men from thinking on the danger he sung them a merry Highland song. About nine or ten o'clock the same night they landed at a place in Sky called Nicolson's Rock, near Scorobreck, in Troternish. In rowing along they found the coast very bad and dangerous, and when they came to the Rock, the Prince was the third man that jump'd out among the water and cried out, 'Take care of the boat, and hawl her up to dry ground,' which was immediately done, he himself assisting as much as any one of them. The Prince had upon him a large big coat, which was become very heavy and cumbersome by the waves beating so much upon it, for it was wet through and through. Captain MacLeod proposed taking the big coat to carry it, for the rock was steep and of a very uneasy ascent. But the Prince would not part with the coat, wet as it was, alleging he was as able to carry it as the Captain was. They went forwards to a cow-byre on the rock, about two miles from Scorobreck, a gentleman's house. In this byre the Prince took up his quarters, the whole company still attending him. Here they took some little refreshment of bread and cheese they had along with them, the cakes being mouldered into very small crumbs. Captain MacLeod intreated the Prince to put on a dry shirt and to take some sleep; but he continued sitting in his wet cloaths, and did not then incline to sleep. However at last he began to nap a little, and would frequently start in his sleep, look briskly up, and stare boldly in the face of every one of them as if he had been to fight them. Upon his waking he would sometimes cry out, 'O Poor England! O Poor England!'

Small Rain

The rain – it was a little rain – walked through the wood
                                        (a little wood)
Leaving behind unexpected decorations and delicacies
On the fox by the dyke, that was eating a salmon's head.
(The poacher who had hidden it wasn't going to be pleased.)

The rain whisperingly went on, past the cliff all Picasso'd
With profiles, blackening the Stoer peat stacks, silvering
Forty sheep's backs, half smudging out a buzzard.
It reached us. It passed us, totally unimpressed.

Not me, I looked at you, all cobwebby with seeds of water,
Changed from Summer to Spring. I had absolutely no way of saying
How vivid can be unemphatic, how bright can be brighter
Than brightness. You knew, though. You were smiling, and no wonder.

Norman MacCaig, b1910

from In search of Scotland

There is no sunlight in the poetry of exile. There is only mist, wind, rain, the cry of whaups, and the slow clouds above damp moorland. That is the real Scotland; that is the Scotland whose memory wrings the withers of the far-from-home; and, in some way that is mysterious, that is the Scotland that even a stranger learns to love.

* * *

It was a wet day. The clouds hung so low over the hills that it seemed possible to stand on a chair and touch them with a stick. The thin rain came slanting down in successive windy sheets, wild gusts flung themselves round corners and appeared to be cast upward into the air again by the violence of the wind. The whole country-side seemed prostrate in grief. There are days like this in Scotland when earth and sky abandon themselves in sorrow. Against the background of a weeping earth and a tearful sky the cheerful good nature of the people is flung in brilliant relief. Fires never look brighter in inn parlours, never comes with more seductive softness that voice asking:

'Will ye take an egg to your tea?'

* * *

In the fading light of late afternoon I came to a loch, silver-white under a grey sky. It was whipped into waves at the edges and pricked all over with falling rain. A man, standing in a little boat and wearing a glassy oilskin, cast a methodical fly on the water, whipping the loch neatly down the wind. Against the sheet of quicksilver I could see the minute black dots of his cast riding the ripples. It was a perfect day for him: rain and wind and cloud.

H V Morton, 1892-1979

from A Description of the Western Islands of Scotland

John Fake who lives in Pabble in the Parish of Kilmoor, alias St Mary's, is constantly troubled with a great Sneezing a day or two before Rain; and if the Sneezing be more than usual, the Rain is said to be the greater therefore he is call'd the Rain-Almanack. He has had this Faculty nine Years past.

Martin Martin, c1660-1719

A golfing party relishing the rain, Islay, 1892. SEA

from Son of Adam

Communal outings were less frequent and usually took the form of picnics. The house party of up to twenty people would pile into cars and drive a dozen miles or so to one of the picnic spots favoured by my mother. She was an enthusiast for picnics, nearly all the other adults disliked them. It was often windy, sometimes wet and always cold. The food was excruciating, huge slabs of bread with ham or cheese between them, cold pieces of congealed mutton, dry crummy cakes, ginger pop and apples. Someone would try to erect a wind break. Someone else would try to light a fire. A child would fall into a stream. Another child would be sick. As the shivering adults cowered on rugs with mackintoshes over their heads you could hear my mother's clear soprano ringing out 'It doesn't matter what the weather is like, there's nothing like a picnic, is there ?'

Denis Forman, b1917

Mull Weather

It rained and rained and rained and rained
    The average was well maintained
And when our fields were simply bogs
    It started raining cats and dogs
After a drought of half an hour
    There came a most refreshing shower
And then the queerest thing of all
    A gentle rain began to fall

Next day 'twas pretty fairly dry
    Save for a deluge from the sky
This wetted people to the skin
    But after that the rain set in
We wondered what's the next we'd get
    As sure as fate we got more wet
But soon we'll have a change again
    And we shall have
            A drop of rain

A summer visitor
first published in the *Oban Times*

If the oak afore the ash,
Then we're gaun to hae a splash.
If the ash afore the oak,
Then we're gaun to hae a soak.

Traditional

from *Journal of Travel in the North of England*
and Scotland, 1704

17 April 1704

And so came to Lockerby, a small town where I lay. It had rained all this day from before noon till night ; and to comfort me more, the room wherein I was to lay was overflown with water, so that the people layd heaps of turf for me to tread upon, to get from the door to the fireplace, and from hence to bed ; and the floor was so worn in holes, that had I tred aside a turf, I might have sunk up to my knees in mud and water ; and no better room was to be had in this town.

Author unknown

from *Upper Annandale : its History and Traditions*

'Let spades and shools do what they may,
Dryfe will hae Drysdale kirk away.'

This saying has proved true. There is but a small portion of the old churchyard, the rest being swept away. In 1670 the church and the greater part of the church-yard were swept away with a flood. Next year a new church was built. But it and the graveyard were carried slowly off to join the others at the sandbank. The Lockerbie people, therefore, built a church out of harm's way.

There is a tradition of a 'joyful widower' who took a second wife, and was leading her proudly home. As they were about to cross the swollen Dryfe, what was his horror to see the open coffin of his first wife come sailing along, and the dead eyes look up at him.

Agnes Marchbank, fl1891-1901

from *Annals of the Parish*

In the month of October, when the corn was yet in the holms, and on the cold land by the river-side, the water of Irville swelled to a great speat, from bank to brae, sweeping all before it, and roaring, in its might, like an agent of divine displeasure sent forth to punish the inhabitants of the earth. The loss of the victual was a thing reparable, and those that suffered did not greatly complain; for, in other respects, their harvest had been plenteous; but the river, in its fury, not content with overflowing the lands, burst through the sandy hills with a raging force, and a riving asunder of the solid ground, as when the fountains of the great deep were broken up. All in the parish was afoot, and on the hills, some weeping and wringing their hands not knowing what would happen, when they beheld the landmarks of the waters deserted, and the river breaking away through the country, like the warhorse set loose in his pasture, and glorying in his might. By this change in the way and channel of the river, all the mills in our parish were left more than half a mile from dam or lade; and the farmers through the whole winter, till the new mills were built, had to travel through a heavy road with their victual, which was a great grievance, and added not a little to the afflictions of this unhappy year.

Aftermath of floods, Lochearn c1910. SEA

John Galt, 1779-1839

from An Account of the Great Floods of August 1829 in the Province of Moray

The heat in the province of Moray, during the months of May, June, and July 1829, was unusually great; and, in the earlier part of that period, the drought was so excessive as to kill many of the recently planted shrubs and trees. As the season advanced, the fluctuations of the barometer became very remarkable. But the usual alternations of weather did not always follow these oscillations: it often happened that the results were precisely the reverse of its prognostications, and observers of the instrument began to lose all confidence in it. That these apparent derangements arose from certain electrical changes in the atmosphere, there can be little doubt. The aurora borealis appeared with uncommon brilliance about the beginning of July, and was frequently seen afterwards, being generally accompanied by windy and unsteady weather, the continued drought having been already interrupted during the previous month by sudden falls of rain, partaking of the character of waterspouts.

A very remarkable instance of one of these occurred on Sunday the 12th of July, at Kean-loch-luichart, a little Highland hamlet, at the head of the lake of that

Family marooned by the floods of August 1829.

W.H.Lizars sculp.

name, in the parish of Contin, in Ross-shire. The innkeeper of Auchanault, having taken shelter under an arch, suddenly beheld a moving mountain of soil, stones, and trees, coming slowly but steadily down the deep worn course of the little stream. He fled in terror. It reached the bridge, where its progress was for a moment arrested; when bursting the feeble barrier that opposed it, on it rushed in dreadful devastation over the plain that bordered the lake below. It was church time. The children left at home were amusing themselves out of doors, and were miraculously preserved by escaping to a hillock ere the ruin reached the spot. An insignificant rivulet, running to the west of the village, was so suddenly swollen, that the people coming from church found great difficulty in passing it. But, as they were on their way towards the larger stream, 300 yards to the eastward, they were alarmed by the fall of the bridge at some distance above the village.

In an instant they found themselves between two impassable torments, and they had barely time to save their lives by crowding to an elevated spot, where they remained till the waters subsided. The whole fury of the flood rushed directly against their devoted houses, and these, and every thing they contained, were at once annihilated, as well as their crops, together with the very soil they grew on;

and, after the debacle had passed away, the course of the burn ran through the ruined hearths of this so recently happy community. This waterspout did not extend beyond two miles on each side of the village, a circumstance that led these simple people to consider their calamity as a visitation of Providence for their landlord's vote in Parliament in favour of Catholic emancipation.

Sir Thomas Dick Lauder, 1784-1848

from The Journal of Thomas Moore

16 April 1821

A French writer mentions, as a proof of Shakespear's attention to particulars, his allusion to climate in Scotland in the words, 'Hail, hail, all hail!' ….

Thomas Moore, 1779-1852

from Macbeth

ACT I, Sc i
[*Witch*]
    When shall we three meet again ?
    In thunder, lightning, or in rain ?

ACT II, Sc iii
[*Lennox*]
    The night has been unruly. Where we lay,
    Our chimneys were blown down ; and, as they say,
    Lamentings heard i' the air, strange screams of death,
    And prophesying, with accents terrible,
    Of dire combustion and confus'd events
    New hatch'd to th' woeful time ; the obscure bird
    Clamour'd the livelong night. Some say the earth was fever-
    ous and did shake.

[*Macbeth*]
    'Twas a rough night.

William Shakespeare, 1564-1616

    Tha 'n cat 's an luath, thig frasan fuar.
    The cat's in the ashes, it's going to rain.

Gaelic proverb

The Tay Bridge Disaster

28 December 1879

Terrible accident on bridge. One or more of high girders blown down. Am not sure as to the safety of last train down from Edinburgh. Will advise further as soon as can be obtained.

Taybridge Station Master James Smith's telegram to
North British Railway Company, Portobello

from Illustrated London News

3 January 1880

The year 1879 has characteristically closed with 'an appalling calamity'. It has been, as all will remember, a year of continuous gloom .... Between Christmas Day and New-Year's Day a frightful, and we may say unprecedented, catastrophe occurred to make the closing twelve months memorable in all future time. Language appears to be utterly incompetent to describe the tragical event, even so far as it is known. A railway train, containing, it is conjectured, about a hundred souls, suddenly disappeared, and not one of its passengers is alive to tell the tale of its disappearance. The train was from Edinburgh to Dundee. The night was tempestuous beyond anything that can be remembered even in the district where

Steam launches and divers' barge used by the searchers after the Tay Bridge Disaster. Illustrated London News 10 January 1880

the accident occurred. The Tay bridge had to be crossed before the train could reach its destination. The Bridge has been regarded as the last and greatest triumph of engineering skill. While a train was passing on Sunday evening, the hurricane swept down upon it with irresistible force. We know no more. We only know that about three thousand feet of the bridge gave way before the blast, and the train with its living freight was precipitated into the tumultuous waters below. Such was the roar of the elements that the noise occasioned by the disaster was completely overborne; and, for some little time, it remained uncertain at Dundee whether the train had ventured on its perilous way. The terrible fact, however, was but too soon ascertained.

from The Tay Bridge Disaster

'Twas about seven o'clock at night,
And the wind it blew with all its might,
And the rain came pouring down,
And the dark clouds seem'd to frown,
And the Demon of the air seem'd to say-
'I'll blow down the Bridge of Tay.'

When the train left Edinburgh
The passengers' hearts were light and felt no sorrow,
But Boreas blew a terrific gale,
Which made their hearts for to quail,
And many of the passengers with fear did say-
'I hope God will send us safe across the Bridge of Tay.'

But when the train came near to Wormit Bay,
Boreas he did loud and angry bray,
And shook the central girders of the Bridge of Tay
On the last Sabbath day of 1879,
Which will be remember'd for a very long time.

So the train sped on with all its might,
And Bonnie Dundee soon hove in sight,
And the passengers' hearts felt light,
Thinking they would enjoy themselves on the New Year,
With their friends at home they lov'd most dear,
And wish them all a happy New Year.

So the train mov'd slowly along the Bridge of Tay,
Until it was about midway,
Then the central girders with a crash gave way,
And down went the train and passengers into the Tay!
The Storm Field did loudly bray,
Because ninety lives had been taken away,
On the last Sabbath day of 1879,
Which will be remember'd for a very long time.

As soon as the catastrophe came to be known
The alarm from mouth to mouth was blown,
And the cry rang out all o'er the town,
Good Heavens! The Tay Bridge is blown down,
And a passenger train from Edinburgh,
Which fill'd all the people's hearts with sorrow,
And made them for to turn pale,
Because none of the passengers were sav'd to tell the tale
How the disaster happen'd on the last Sabbath day of 1879,
Which will be remember'd for a very long time.

It must have been an awful sight,
To witness in the dusky moonlight
While the Storm Fiend did laugh and angry did bray,
Along the Railway Bridge of the Silv'ry Tay.
Oh! Ill-fated Bridge of the Silvr'y Tay,
I must now conclude my lay
By telling the world fearlessly without the least dismay,
That your central girders would not have given way,
At least many sensible men do say,
Had they been supported on each side with buttresses,
At least many a sensible man confesses,
For the stronger we our houses do build,
The less chance we have of being killed.

William McGonagall, 1825-1902

The broken bridge from the north. Illustrated
London News 10 January 1880

On the arrival in Scotland of Mary, Queen of Scots,

19 August 1561

The very face of the heaven at the time of her arrival, did manifestly speak what comfort was brought into this country with her, to wit, sorrow, dolor, darkness, and all impiety; for in the memory of man, that day of the year was never seen a more dolorous face of the heaven, than was at her arrival, which two days after did so continue: for besides the surface wet, and corruption of the air, the mist was so thick and dark, that scarce might any man espy another the length of two pair of butts; the sun was not seen to shine two days before, nor two days after. That forewarning gave God unto us but alas the most part were blind.

John Knox, c 1513-1572

Darkness on land and sea.
Dave Reed

from A Diary of Public Transactions and Other Occurrences Chiefly in Scotland

Upone the 28 of Maii 1650, thair rayned bluid, be the space of thrie myles, in the Erle of Bukcleuchis boundis, upon the landis of —— neir to the Englische bordouris; quhilk wes verifeyit in presence of the Committee of Stait.

John Nicoll, c1590-1667

from Letters from Edinburgh written in the years 1774 and 1775

The natives of this Country, who have travelled much in warmer climates, tell you, that Scotland is far colder than England, and you cannot clothe yourself too warmly in winter. As to myself, I have not as yet found any of these precautions necessary, and I wear just the same number of cloaths I should do in England at this season of the year.

North Bridge, Edinburgh. Sam Bough

Though this winter has hitherto been very mild, I can easily perceive that the weather is much more changeable than it is in England, and that frequently you experience all the seasons in one day. In the middle of it, when the Sun is in his meridian, the heat is sometimes extremely powerful; and in the evening you have all that piercing cold you might expect here in winter...

The most particular effect which I find of this Climate, is the Winds; which here reign in all their violence, and seem indeed to claim the country as their own. A person, who has passed all his time in England, cannot be said to know what a wind is: he has zephyrs, and breezes, and gales, but nothing more; at least they appear so to me after having felt the hurricanes of Scotland.

Dr James Graham going along the North Bridge in a high wind. Kay's Portraits

As this Town is situated on the borders of the sea, and surrounded by hills of immense height, the currents of air are carried down between them with a rapidity and a violence that nothing can resist. It has frequently been known, that in the New Town of Edinburgh three or four people have scarce been able to shut the door of the house... Not many days ago an Officer... a man of six feet high, and, one would imagine, by no means calculated to become the sport of winds, was, however, in following another gentleman out of the Castle, lifted up by their violence from the ground, carried over his companion's head, and thrown at some distance on the stones. This, I can assure you, is a literal fact. At other times, the winds, instead of rushing down with impetuosity, whirl about in eddies, and become still more dreadful. On these occasions it is almost impossible to stir out of doors, as the dust and stones gathered up in these vortices not only prevent your seeing, but frequently cut your legs by the velocity with which they are driven. The Scots have a particular appellation for this, The Stour.

The chief scene where these winds exert their influence, is the New Bridge, which, by being thrown over a long valley that is open at both ends, and particularly from being balustraded on each side, admits the wind in the most charming manner imaginable; and you receive it with the same force you would do, were it conveyed to you through a pair of bellows. It is far from unentertaining for a man to pass over this bridge on a tempestuous day. In walking over it this morning I had the pleasure of adjusting a lady's petticoats which had blown almost entirely over her head, and which prevented her disengaging herself from the situation she was in: but in charity to her distresses, I concealed her charms from public view: one poor gentleman, who was rather too much engaged with the novelty of the objects before him, unfortunately forgot his own hat and wig, which were lifted up by an unpremeditated puff, and carried entirely away.

Edward Topham, 1751-1820

from Caller Oysters

> Whan big as burns the gutters rin
> Gin ye hae catch a droukit skin,
> To *Luckie Middlemist's* loup in,
>   And sit fu' snug
> O'er oysters and a dram o'gin,
>   Or haddock lug.

Robert Fergusson, 1750-1774

from Edinburgh: Picturesque Notes

A Scot of poetic temperament, and without religious exhaltation, drops as if by nature into the public house. The picture may not be pleasing; but what else is a man to do in this dog's weather?

Robert Louis Stevenson, 1850-1894

Postcard to Duncan Grant

27 June 1938

Skye is often raining, but also fine: hardly; semi-transparent; like living in a jelly fish lit up with green light.

Virginia Woolf, 1882-1941

from Letter to Dorothy Brett

14 August 1928

So this is your Scotland. It is rather nice, but dampish and Northern and one shrinks a trifle inside one's skin. For these countries one should be an amphibian.

D H Lawrence, 1885-1930

Black Islands near Kyle of Lochalsh. Harry Williams

from To Circumjack Cencastrus

Scotland's cauld and grey, you say,
But it's no ill to prove
Oor dourest hills are only
Rainbows at a'e remove.

Hugh MacDiarmid, 1892-1978

from Letter to Washington Irving, 1817

This is a lachrymose climate, evermore showering. We, however, are children of
the mist and must not mind a little whimpering of the clouds.

Sir Walter Scott, 1771-1832

from Tea and Biscuits

Begin with a town in the East; the North and the East; a Scottish town. Here, they have fogs in the morning, salty dry and cold in the throat, that hold your breath. Some days the mist will be gone by lunchtime. Some days you will turn down a street and stand to see the river and a lake of white will be on it; a milk fog, deep above the water, with nothing but the blue of a hilltop or bare sky to show the other side. The mist nestles there, on the cold water, hiding from the town and you; biding its time for the other days, when it will wrap around the houses and stay. Then you will drive through nights that are yellow, full of glimpses of things you should recognise, things that run at you while you squeeze along tunnels of light.

Begin with a night like that. No stars.

A L Kennedy, b1965

from *The Private Memoirs and Confessions of a Justified Sinner*

He seated himself on the pinnacle of the rocky precipice, a little within the top of the hill to the westward, and, with a light and buoyant heart, viewed the beauties of the morning, and inhaled its salubrious breeze. 'Here,' thought he, 'I can converse with nature without disturbance, and without being intruded on by any appalling or obnoxious visitor.' The idea of his brother's dark and malevolent looks coming at that moment across his mind, he turned his eyes instinctively to the right, to the point where that unwelcome guest was wont to make his appearance. Gracious Heaven! What an apparition was there presented to his view! He saw, delineated in the cloud, the shoulders, arms, and features of a human being of the most dreadful aspect. The face was the face of his brother, but dilated to twenty times the natural size. Its dark eyes gleamed on him through the mist, while every furrow of its hideous brow frowned deep as the ravines on the brow of the hill. George started, and his hair stood up in bristles as he gazed on this horrible monster. He saw every feature, and every line of the face, distinctly, as it gazed on him with an intensity that was hardly brookable. Its eyes were fixed on him, in the same manner as those of some carnivorous animal fixed on its prey; and yet there was fear and trembling, in these unearthly features, as plainly depicted as murderous malice. The giant apparition seemed sometimes to be cowering down as in terror, so that nothing but its brow and eyes were seen; still these never turned one moment from their object – again it rose imperceptibly up, and began to approach with great caution; and as it neared, the dimensions of its form lessened, still continuing, however, far above the natural size.

James Hogg, 1770-1835

from *A Hatchment*

When all is ready for them, the mists sweep down and cover everything from the interior of the darkness comes the cries of wild ducks, of herons, as they sit upon the trees, and of geese passing overhead. Inside the wreaths of mist another world seems to have come into existence, something distinct from and antagonistic to mankind. When the mist once descends, blotting out the familiar features of the landscape, leaving perhaps the Rock of Stirling floating in the air, the three black trees upon the bare rock of the Fairy Hill growing from nothing, or

Ben Arthur, 'The Cobbler'.

Tarbet and 'The Cobbler' – Loch Lomond. SEA

the peak of the Cobbler, seeming to peer above enormous mountain ranges, though in reality nothing more vast than the long shoulder of Ben Lomond intervenes, the change has come that gives Menteith its special character.

There are mists all the world over, and in Scotland in particular; mists circling round the Western Islands, filling the glens and boiling in the corries of the hills; mists that creep out of the sea or in towards the land from seawards, threatening and dreadful-looking; but none like ours, so impalpable and strange, and yet so fitting to our low, flat mosses with our encircling hills. In older days they sheltered the marauders from the north, who in their gloom fell on the valley as if they had sprung from the night, plundered and burned and harried, and then retreated under cover of the mist, back to their fastnesses.

R B Cunninghame Graham, 1852-1936

Auld mune mist,
Ne'er dee'd o' thrist.

Traditional

Mists over Glen Affric. Laurie Campbell

from The English Notebooks

Inversnaid, 3 July – Last night seemed to close in clear, and even at midnight it was still light enough to read; but this morning rose on us misty and chill, with spattering showers of rain. Clouds momentarily settled and shifted on the hill-tops, shutting us in even more completely than these steep and rugged green walls would be sure to do, even in the clearest weather. Often these clouds came down and enveloped us in a drizzle, or rather a shower, of such minute drops that they had not weight enough to fall. This, I suppose, was a genuine Scotch mist; and as such it is well enough to have experienced it, though I would willingly never see it again.

Nathaniel Hawthorne, 1804-1864

from The Curse of Minerva

A land of meanness, sophistry, and mist.

George Gordon, Lord Byron, 1788-1824

from Visitors' book of Ben Nevis Hotel

Roll by, thou dense and damp pea-soupy shroud!
Do we thus reach the highest point in vain?
Roll by! we say, and leave behind no cloud
Our view to mar; but, should'st thou still remain,
Mark well the threat – 'Never shall we come again.'

If at first you don't succeed, try again:
Mist and rain you should not heed, try again;
When the clouds have rolled away,
And the sun holds glorious sway,
Climb the path without delay, come again,
All your labours he'll repay – grand old Ben.

We climbed thy stony sides, oh Ben!
We groped around thy cloudy head,
We peered, and jeered, and swore – and then,
In sheer disgust, we went to bed.

We toiled along with saddened hearts – and grief,
And found- ah, well, just mist and tinned Australian beef.

late 19th century

from History of the Worthies of England

A Scottish mist may wet an Englishman to the skin, – that is, small mischiefs in the beginning, if not seasonably prevented, may prove very dangerous.

Thomas Fuller, 1608-1661

Is trom snithe air tigh gun tubhadh.
Rain-drops come heavy on a house unthatched.

Gaelic proverb

A cloudy blue sky near Glasgow.

from Greenvoe

In the endless bestiary of the weather the unicorns of cloud are littered far west in the Atlantic; the sun their sire, the sea their dame. Swiftly they hatch and flourish. They travel eastwards, a grey silent stampeding herd. Their shining hooves beat over the Orkneys and on out into the North Sea. Sometimes it takes days for that migration to pass. But many are torn on the crags and hills, and spill their precious ichor on the farmlands. Crofters wake to cornfields and pastures extravagantly jewelled.

George Mackay Brown, b1921

Lochain na h'Achlaise, Rannoch Moor.

from The Thirty-Nine Steps

Almost five o'clock the carriage had emptied, and I was left alone as I had hoped. I got out at the next station, a little place whose name I scarcely noted, set right in the heart of a bog. It reminded me of one of those forgotten little stations in the Karroo. An old stationmaster was digging in his garden, and with his spade over his shoulder sauntered to the train, took charge of a parcel, and went back to his potatoes. A child of ten received my ticket, and I emerged on a white road that straggled over the brown moor.

It was a gorgeous spring evening, with every hill showing as clear as cut amethyst. The air had the queer, rooty smell of bogs, but it was as fresh as mid-ocean, and it had the strangest effect on my spirits. I actually felt light-hearted. I might have been a boy out for a spring holiday tramp, instead of a man of thirty-seven very much wanted by the police. I felt just as I used to feel when I was starting for a big trek on a frosty morning on the high veld. If you believe me, I swung along that road whistling. There was no plan of campaign in my head, only just to go on and on in this blessed, honest-smelling hill country, for every mile put me in a better humour with myself.

John Buchan, 1875-1940

from The Weatherhouse

Infinite sky was over him, blue land ran on and on until it seemed itself a ruffled fold of sky, a quivering of light upon the air; the blue sea trembled on the boundaries of space; and the man standing there alone was rapt up into the infinitudes around, lost for awhile the limitations of himself. He came back slowly. Strange how the land could be transfigured! A blue April morning, the shimmer of light, a breath, a passing air, and it was no longer a harsh and stubborn country, its hard-won fields beleaguered by moor and whin, its stones heaped together in dyke and cairn, marking the land like lines upon a weathered countenance, whose past must stay upon it to the end; but a dream, willing men's hearts. In the sun the leafless boughs were gleaming. Birches were like tangles of shining hair; or rather, he thought, insubstantial, floating like shredded light above the soil. Below the hills blue floated in the hollows, all but tangible, like a distillation that light had set free from the earth; and on a rowan tree in early leaf, its boughs blotted against the background, the tender leaves, like flakes of green fire, floated too, the wild burning life of spring loosened from earth's control. On every side earth was transmuted. Scents floated, the subtle life released from earth and assailing the pulses. Songs floated. The dour and thankless country, this land that *grat a' winter and girned a' summer* could change before one's eyes to an elfin and enchanted radiance, could look, by some rare miracle of light or moisture, essentialised.

Nan Shepherd, 1893-1981

Sheddaes

Sheddaes dinna shaw on dreich days,
rain, cowpin owre causies
drouns the hale street.
Trees hing tuim on lanely braes
bydin for the sin.
Wee burds, aye cheery
cheip cheip frae drouthy howfs an
luikin doun, nae brichtness maks its mark.
Bit syne the cluds birl awa
an oot cums yersel.
Trees steir theirsels an wag a haun.
The wee burds blether an lauch the lift
while keekin doun, ma sheddae finds itsel
ance mair tethert tae ma taes.

Donald C Farquhar b1938

The Comin' o' the Spring

There's no a muir in my ain land but's fu' o' sang the day,
Wi' the whaup, and the gowden plover, and the lintie upon the brae.
The birk in the glen is springin', the rowan tree in the shaw,
And every burn is rinnin' wild wi' the meltin' o' the snaw.

The wee white cluds in the blue lift, are hurryin' light and free,
Their shadows flee on the hills, where I, too, fain wad be;
The wind frae the west is blawin', and wi' it seems to bear
The scent o' the thyme and gowan, thro' a' the caller air.

The herd doon the hillside's linkin' o licht his heart may be
Whose step is on the heather, his glance ower muir and lea !
On the moss are the wild deuks gath'rin', whar the pules like diamonds lie,
And far up soar the wild geese, wi' weird, unyirdly cry.

In mony a neuk the primrose lies hid frae stranger e'en,
An' the broom on the knowes is wavin', wi' its cludin o' gowd and green;
Ower the first green sprigs o' the heather, the muir fowl faulds his wing
And there's nought but joy in my ain land, at the comin' o' the Spring.

Lady John Scott, 1811-1900

Sunny, sunny shower
Come on for half an hour,
Gar a' the hens cour,
Gar a' the hare's clap,
Gar ilka wife o'Lammermoor,
Put on her kail-pat.

Rainbow, rainbow, haud away hame,
A' your bairns are dead but ane,
And it lies sick at yon grey stane,
And will be dead ere ye win hame ;
Gang owre the Drumaw and yont the lea,
And down by the side o'yonder sea,
Your bairn lies greetin' like to die,
And the big tear-drap is in his ee.

Traditional

from *Gallery of Nature*

The summer of 1679 was extremely hot. It is related, that one of the minions of tyranny, who in that calamitous period harassed the poor presbyterians in Scotland with captious questions, having asked a shepherd in Fife, whether the killing of the notorious Sharp, Archbishop of St Andrews, which had happened in May, was murder; he replied, that he could not tell, but there had been fine weather ever since.

Rev Thomas Milner, d1882

from *Memoir of the Reverend Sydney Smith*
by Lady Holland

No nation has so large a stock of benevolence as the Scotch. Their temper stands anything but an attack on their climate. They would even have you believe they can ripen fruit; and to be candid, I must own in remarkably warm summers, I have tasted peaches that made excellent pickles.

Sydney Smith, 1771-1845

from *The Cherrie and the Slae*

The dew as diamonds did hing
Upon the tender twistis ying
Owre-twinkling all the trees ;
And aye where flours did flourish fair,
There suddenly I saw repair
Ane swarm of sounding bees.
Some sweetly has the honey socht,
Whill they were cloggit sore;
Some willingly the wax has wrocht,
To keep it up in store.
So heaping, with keeping,
Into their hives they hide it,
Precisely and wisely
For winter they provide it.

Alexander Montgomerie, c1545-1597

In the Orchard. Edward Atkinson Hornel

from The Diary of a Canny Man 1818-28

Fyvie, 26 June, 1826

Have had John Ogilvie yesterday and this day cutting hay. It is not above a half or a third of a crop, it is so terribly burnt with the drought. Corn and bear crops are also suffering severely now. Corn is shooting and not above four or five inches long; bear much the same. On some hard high lying spots the crops are dried up with the great heat to a cinder.

27 June, 1826

Butter is softer than I ever remember to see it. Can scarcely be prevented turning into oil. The heat continues to be strong in the extreme. The roads are deep with dust and a cart, when there is the least wind, has always a cloud of dust about her.

28 June, 1826

Have had some terrible loud thunder this afternoon, which was followed by a heavy shower of rain, which is very agreeable after such a burning heat and drought.

Leading sheaves on a hill farm. Scotland Illustrated, SEA

29 June, 1826

From the *Journal* it appears the heat of the sun was so great in high districts of the county as to set on fire whins in many places.

1 July, 1826

This day has been remarkable for thunder. Throughout the whole day has kept pretty distant round our horizon until towards night about 8 o'clock when it came above our heads with tremendous claps.

5 July, 1826

Read the *Journal* – accounts of great thunder storms in different parts of the country. Some buildings and beasts injured, but as yet have not heard of any loss of human life. There seems also to be great devastation by the burning of moss and muirs from the head of Don along by the source of Dee, said to be from one to two hundred square miles.

Adam Mackie , 1788-1850

from The Cone Gatherers

It was a good tree by the sea-loch, with many cones and much sunshine; it was homely too, with rests among its topmost branches as comfortable as chairs.

For hours the two men had worked in silence there, a hundred feet from the earth, closer, it seemed, to the blue sky round which they had watched the sun slip. Misted in the morning, the loch had gone through many shades of blue and now was mauve, like the low hills on its far side. Seals that had been playing tag in and out of the seaweed under the surface had disappeared round the point, like children gone home for tea. A destroyer has steamed seawards, with a sailor singing cheerfully. More sudden and swifter than hawks, and roaring louder than waterfalls, aeroplanes had shot down from the sky over the wood, whose autumnal colours they seemed to have copied for camouflage. In the silence that had followed gunshots had cracked far off in the wood.

From the tall larch could be glimpsed, across the various-tinted crowns of the trees, the chimneys of the mansion behind its private fence of giant silver firs. Neil, the elder of the brothers, had often paused, his hand stretched out from its ragged sleeve to pluck the sweet resinous cones, and gazed at the great house with a calm yet bitter intentness and anticipation, as if, having put a spell on it, he was waiting for it to change. He never said what he expected or why he watched; nor did his brother ever ask.

Scots pines by Loch Laggan. Charles Tait

For Calum the tree-top was interest enough; in it he was as indigenous as a squirrel or bird. His black curly hair was speckled with orange needles; his torn jacket was stained green, as was his left knee visible through a hole rubbed in his trousers. Chaffinches fluttered round him, ignoring his brother; now and then one would alight on his head or shoulder. He kept chuckling to them, and his sunburnt face was alert and beautiful with trust. Yet he was a much faster gatherer than his brother, and reached far out to where the brittle branches drooped and creaked under his weight. Neil would sometimes glance across to call out: 'Careful.' It was the only word spoken in the past two hours.

The time came when, thrilling as a pipe lament across the water, daylight announced it must go: there was a last blaze of light, an uncanny clarity, a splendour and puissance; and then the abdication began. Single stars appeared, glittering in a sky pale and austere. Dusk like a breathing drifted in among the trees and crept over the loch. Slowly the mottled yellow of the chestnuts, the bronze of beech, the saffron of birches, all the magnificent sombre harmonies of decay, became indistinguishable. Owls hooted. A fox barked.

Robin Jenkins, b1912

from The Steamie

[*Mrs Culfeathers*]   Ah kin aye mind, as a wee lassie, gaun wi' ma mother, and d'y'e know whit was lovely? Seein' Glesca Green wi' aw the washin' hingin fae the lines. Yon was a marvellous sight.

[*Doreen*]   Doesnae sound aw that marvellous tae me.

[*Mrs Culfeathers*]   Ach, ye should have seen it hen, especially in the summer time. Of course we had real summers then, fae May right ontae September. It was that hot the tar used tae stick tae yer feet, and the whole of Glesca Green was like a sea of colour, sheets and mattress covers and the men's shirts. White as snow as far as ye could see, and lovely coloured silks and woollens, aw dancin' in the dryin' wind.

At that age ah always thought they looked kinna happy, it sounds daft ah know hen, but it was the men's shirts and women's dresses. Ye see, they aw have arms and when the wind blew them aboot, they aw seemed tae be wavin' tae each other. It wis as if the claes had a life o' their ain. Ah aye mind o' that, and underneath them the women were aw movin' aboot, laughin' and jokin' wi' wan another … it was noisy but tae me then, somehow … thrillin'.

Tony Roper, b1941

from Kidnapped

It was now high day, cloudless, and very hot. The valley was as clear as in a picture. About half a mile up the water was a camp of redcoats; a big fire blazed in their midst, at which some were cooking; and near by, on the top of a rock about as high as ours, there stood a sentry, with the sun sparkling on his arms. All the way down along the riverside were posted other sentries; here near together, there widelier scattered; some planted like the first, on places of command, some of the ground level and marching and counter-marching so as to meet half way. Higher up the glen, where the ground was more open, the chain of posts was continued by horse-soldiers, whom we could see in the distance riding to and fro. Lower down, the infantry continued; but as the stream was suddenly swelled by the confluence of a considerable burn, they were more widely set, and only watched the fords and stepping-stones.

I took but one look at them and ducked again into my place. It was strange indeed to see this valley, which had lain so solitary in the hour of dawn, bristling with arms and dotted with the red coats and breeches.

'Ye see,' said Alan, 'this was what I was afraid of, Davie: that they would watch the burnside. They began to come in about two hours ago, and, man! but ye're a grand hand at the sleeping! We're in a narrow place. If they get up the sides of the hill they could easy spy us with a glass; but if they'll only keep in the foot of the valley, we'll do it yet. The posts are thinner down the water: and, come night, we'll try our hand at getting by them.'

'And what are we to do till night?' I asked.

'Lie here', says he, 'and birstle.'

That one good Scots word 'birstle', was indeed the most of the story of the day that we had to pass. You are to remember that we lay on the bare top of a rock, like scones upon a girdle; the sun beat upon us cruelly; the rock grew so heated, a man could scarce endure the touch of it; and the little patch of earth and fern, which kept cooler, was only large enough for one at a time. We took it turn about to lie on the naked rock, which was indeed like the position of that saint that was martyred on a gridiron; and it ran in my mind how strange it was, that in the same climate and at only a few days' distance, I should have suffered so cruelly, first from the cold upon my island and now from heat upon this rock. ...

All the while we had no water, only raw brandy for a drink, which was worse than nothing; but we kept the bottle as cool as we could, burying it in the earth, and got some relief by bathing our breasts and temples. ...

The tediousness and pain of these hours upon the rock grew only the greater

Swimming in a loch. SEA

as the day went on; the rock getting still the hotter, and the sun fiercer. There were giddiness, and sickness, and sharp pangs like rheumatism to be supported. I minded then, and have often minded since, on the lines in our Scotch psalm:

> The moon by night thee shall not smite,
> Nor yet the sun by day;

and indeed it was only by God's blessing that we were neither of us sun-smitten.

Robert Louis Stevenson, 1850-1894

from Valda's Poem/Sleevenotes

Sleevenotes to Hugh MacDiarmid's record 'Whaur Extremes Meet': 'Recorded at Brownbank, the home of Valda and Chris Grieve, near Biggar in the Lanarkshire hills on two sultry days in June 1978. Chris, in his chair by the window, talking with his friend, the poet Norman MacCaig, a wee dram in every glass. Valda in swimsuit, working in the garden, or keeping the soft-coated Wheaten and Border Terrier quiet for the recording.'

June sun presses on my back as I bend
sweat gathers at my neck and under my arms
I am naked as I can be in my bathing costume

I step out onto the flowerbeds
making light footprints with my bare feet
Spray trails from the watering-can
falls in dark circles round the plants

I want to lie out on the parched grass
and let the sun's hands touch me everywhere
let them finger the frail flesh of my breasts
rub gold into the crease and wrinkle of my stomach

At the open window edged with ivy
they sit, two old men in their shirt-sleeves
On the table between them a bottle of whisky
the two fat volumes of collected poems
and a tape-recorder lapping up their words

The dog flops in the shade of the back door
I go to her when she stirs, stroke her hot fur
give her water, keep her from barking

I hear their talk and laughter, his and Norman's
I hear the rise and fall of Chris's voice
and the rhythms of his favourite poems, over and over

In the afternoon I sit against the apple tree
feeling the dent of bark on my bare shoulders
I close my eyes and the murmur of their voices
blurs with the birdsong that maybe
when we listen to the finished record
will have swum inside the poems

Elizabeth Burns, b1957

Tea in the garden. Robert Miller

from *The Band o' Shearers*

'Twas on an August afternoon,
When folk could spy the harvest moon,
The lads and lasses gathered roun'
　　To talk about the shearing.
I whisper'd Jean if she wad gang,
And shear wi' me the hale day lang,
And join wi' me a merry thrang –
　　A jolly band of shearers.

And should the weather be ower hot
I'll cast my gravat and my coat,
An' help my lass to shear her lot,
　　Amang the band o'shearers.
So, bonnie lassie, will ye gang
And shear wi' me the hale day lang,
I'll cheer ye wi' a hearty sang,
　　Amang the band o' shearers.

Traditional

from *The Island of Sheep*

We all attended the clipping. It was a very hot day, and the air in the fold was thick with the reek of sheep and the strong scent of the keel-pot, from which the shorn beasts were marked with a great L. I have seen a good deal of shearing in my time, but I have never seen it done better than by these Borderers, who wrought in perfect silence and apparently with effortless ease. The Australian sheep-hand may be quicker at the job, but he could not be a greater artist. There was never a gash or a shear-mark, the fleeces dropped plumply beside the stools, and the sheep, no longer dingy and weathered but a dazzling white, were as evenly trimmed as if they had been fine women in the hands of a coiffeur. It was too smelly a place for the ladies to sit in long, but twenty yards off was crisp turf beginning to be crimsoned with bell-heather, and the shingle-beds and crystal waters of the burn. We ended up camping on a little hillock, where we could look down upon the scene, and around to the hills shimmering in the heat, and up to the deep blue sky on which were etched two mewing buzzards.

We had our luncheon there, when the work stopped for the midday rest, and Haraldsen and I went down afterwards to smoke with the herds. The clipping meal at Laverlaw was established by ancient precedent. There was beer for all, but whisky only for the older men. There were crates of mutton pies for which the Hangingshaw baker was famous, and baskets of buttered scones and oatcakes and skim-milk cheese. The company were mighty trenchermen, and I observed the herd of the Back Hill of the Cludden, to whom this was a memorable occasion, put away six pies and enough cakes and cheese to last me for a week.

John Buchan, 1875-1940

from The House of Elrig

Thereafter our journeys to the sea-shore below the lonely Chapel of St. Medan became voyages of discovery. It was always sunshine. We would set off in the only car my mother possessed, a 1914 Ford with brass lamps and radiator – (heated derision of my sister when she claimed to have been driven at a full 30mph along the shore road) – a chauffeur at the wheel, my mother wearing a mauve motoring-veil. We children sat in a row on the folded-down hood, our feet dangling above the back seat, singing and shouting and chattering with anticipation. When we came in sight of the sea from the top of the grass cliffs (called 'heughs' in Galloway, and practically unpronounceable) it looked sparkling like imperfectly smoothed silver-paper; we had our own word for this – 'shinkly' and the shinkli-

Will Strachan, enjoying his piece, in a break from peat cutting in Banffshire, summer 1968. Alexander Fenton, SEA

ness added to our exhilaration because it added even more light and movement to the sky and the salt wind in our faces.

Gavin Maxwell, 1914-1969

NEITHER SUN NOR SEA
can hurt these clothes

These smart little clothes are not cheap. But they are guaranteed absolutely impervious to sun or sea water. Both Jenners and the cloth makers will see that this promise is kept. The kilt outfit costs £4:11:6 for a boy of 5. The coat and cap £3:10:6. Send for further details and garment on approval.

JENNERS
PRINCES STREET EDINBURGH
LIMITED

Fraserburgh, a London & North Eastern Railway poster.
H G Gawthorn

The hairst at Auchendinny in the early nineteenth century.

from A schoolboy's essay book,
Arbuthnott School, 1914

Everything around seemed to acclaim harvest. The wide fields of waving corn, gleaming yellow in the morning sunshine, the sharp click! click! of the binder, the voice of the driver calling his horses, who seem greatly to relish a few mouthfuls of ripe grain and the busy workmen rapidly 'stooking' (I think that's the way you spell it) the sheaves – all of them acclaim the same thing. Zip! Zip! the rain begins to descend with the suddenness of a summer shower, but it soon passes, and the farmer, much relieved to see that it was only a 'bit shoorey' informs the men to 'stick in' again. That is generally the way the first cutting proceeds. Then comes the leading, and although I admire the thistle as Scotland's emblem, I can't say the same of it in connection with 'bigging' a cart.

James Leslie Mitchell (Lewis Grassic Gibbon) 1901-1935

from A Summer on Skye

Summer has leaped suddenly on Edinburgh like a tiger. The air is still and hot above the houses; but every now and then a breath of east wind startles you through the warm sunshine – like a sudden sarcasm felt through a strain of flattery – and passes on detested of every organism. But, with this exception, the atmosphere is so close, so laden with a body of heat, that a thunderstorm would be almost welcomed as a relief. Edinburgh, on her crags, held high towards the sun – too distant the sea to send cool breezes to street and square – is at this moment an uncomfortable dwelling-place. Beautiful as ever, of course – for nothing can be finer than the ridge of the Old Town etched on hot azure – but close, breathless suffocating. Great volumes of white smoke surge out of the railway station; great choking puffs of dust issue from the houses and shops that are being gutted in Princes Street. The Castle Rock is gray; the trees are of a dingy olive; languid 'swells,' arm-in-arm, promenade uneasily the heated pavement;

Promenading beneath Edinburgh Castle Rock.

water-carts everywhere dispense their treasures; and the only human being really to be envied in the city is the small boy who, with trousers tucked up, and unheeding of maternal vengeance, marches coolly in the fringe of the ambulating shower-bath. Oh for one hour of heavy rain! Thereafter would the heavens wear a clear and tender, instead of a dim and sultry hue. Then would the Castle rock brighten in colour, and the trees and grassy slopes doff their dingy olives for the emeralds of April. Then would the streets be cooled, and the dust be allayed. Then would the belts of city verdure, refreshed, pour forth gratitude in balmy smells; and Fife – low-lying across the Forth – break from its hot neutral tint into the greens, purples, and yellows that of right belong to it. But rain won't come; and for weeks, perhaps, there will be nothing but hot sun above, and hot street beneath; and for the respiration of poor human lungs an atmosphere of heated dust, tempered with east wind.

Moreover, one is tired and jaded. The whole man, body and soul, like sweet bells jangled, out of tune, and harsh, is fagged with work, eaten up of impatience, and haunted with visions of vacation.

Alexander Smith, 1830-1867

from Greenvoe

All morning the sun had fought with silent blind blunderings of sea fog for possession of the island. Ivan Westray, sitting on the edge of the pier waiting for his passengers to arrive, watched the struggle of the grey ram and the golden god. Within an hour the weather for the day would be decided, one way or the other. The fog leapt forward suddenly, then retreated as a sword of light shore through its outer fleece; then backed out again till the Skarf's fishing boat *Engels* dipped like a ghost at her moorings. Ivan Westray checked that everything was stowed on board : the mail-bag, the boxes of eggs, the empty gas containers, the black calf tied to the handrail. He lit another cigarette. Presently Mr Joseph Evie in his dark Sunday suit emerged out of the swirls, smiling, and climbed carefully down the ladder into the ferry-boat : he was on his way to the county council meeting in the town. 'Half past eight, Ivan,' he said. Ivan Westray cleaned his finger nails with a burnt match. 'We have to wait,' he said, 'till Johnny's had his oats.' The fog staggered silently against the boat and the pier. The Indian packman, Dewas (Johnny) Singh, stood above them, smiling; he lowered his case to Ivan Westray; turned: and climbed down after it into the *Skua*.

Boats at Ullapool. Charles Tait

[106]

'Hurry up, Casanova,' said Ivan Westray. 'we're late. Button your flies.'

Blue chasms of sky appeared over the neighbouring island of Quoylay. The Sound glittered. The sun smote the nearer waters. The fog turned, fled with one great bound into the Atlantic. The sun possessed the morning. The hill and the village were lapped in warm light. It would be a glorious day.

George Mackay Brown, b1921

Weather words and more

There are some words in this anthology which you may find unfamiliar. Some are no longer current, but a great many are still in use today, perhaps because they describe the different aspects of weather so perfectly. If you have trouble with words that are not on this list, try saying them aloud: the sense will usually become clear.

attery : stormy
bachles : snow stuck to shoes
barber : freezing mist
beer : barley
bicker : patter
bield : shelter
bigg : six-row barley
birsle : to scorch
blashy : rainy
blenter : gusty wind
bub : squall
carry : sky
channlestane : curling stone
coorse : stormy
crameuch : hoarfrost
cuif : lout
cuist : cast
dee : down
dish : rain heavily
dowie : dismal
drackie : misty
draigled : bedraggled
dreep : steady fall of light rain
dribble : drizzle
droukit : drenched
drucken : drunken
drumkie : cloudy
dryachty : inclined to be dry
fell : very
flaff : blow in gusts

flag : large snowflake
freest : frost
gandiegow : heavy shower
gangrel : vagrant
gey : very
glaur : mire
glorgie : sultry
glushie : slushy
goor : slush in running water
gowany : bright
growthie : warm and moist
grumlie : unsettled
gull : cold mist
gurl : roar
hirplin : limping
hogg : yearling sheep
hoo : howl
howlet : owl
hushle : strong wind
jabble : choppy sea
jaup : splashing of the surf
jaw : surge of water
jeel : extreme cold
leesome : fine
laverock ; lark
limmer : hussy
linn : torrent
lintie : linnet
lithesome : gentle
loup : leap

lown : calm
lunkie : sultry
maumie : mild
mirk : dark
muir : moor
muith : humid
neb : beak
nib-nebs : Jack Frost
nizzin : buffeting
peenge : look cold and miserable
peever : hopscotch
pirl : gentle breeze
pish-oot : downpour
plowtery : showery
plype : sudden, heavy shower
pykin : plucking
quair : book or poem
quhen, quhone : when
quhill : will
quhilk : which
quhisling : whistling
raff : short sharp shower
rainin' auld wives and
    pipe stapples : heavy rain
reevin : gusty
remeid : remedy
roukie : muggy
rouline : damp, misty
rumballiach : tempestuous
sapple : soak
scour : shower
shake-wind : a blustery wind in the corn
shockle : icicle
shools : shovels
sic : such

skelpit : hurried
skippie : slippery
smirr : light rain
smoch : thick fog
smochy : close
snawbroo : melted snow
snawwreath : snowdrift
snell : biting
snippin : biting snow
soopit : swept
spleuterie : rainy
spreitis : spirits
starrach : bleak
suggie lan : wet land
sump : a great fall of rain
sweevil : gust of wind
symmer : summer
tangle : icicle
tattery : very windy
tautit : tangled
thirling : piercing cold
thunder-plump : sudden thunder shower
tirl : breeze
tosie : cosy
tousie : blustery
unyirdly : unearthly
ure : damp mist
watergaw : fragmentary rainbow
waukrif : vigilant
wean : child
wersh : raw and cold
whummle : avalanche
yett : gate
yowdendrift : snow driven by wind

Index